GOD'S HELL NOT FOREVER

God's Fulfillment
Of the

HELL'S CAPTIVES RELEASED
(Rev. 20:13-14)

By ROSS MARSHALL
Copyright 2015

GOD'S HELL NOT FOREVER
First Edition, 2015
Reprinted and Published
By R. S. Marshall
First Reprint Edition,

2015 © Ross S. Marshall

ISBN-13. 978-1514232071
ISBN-10: 1514232073

Weirdvideos.com
R. S. Marshall
P. O. Box 1191
Anacortes, WA   98221
www.UniversalAtonement.com
www.weirdvideos.com

Ordering Information:

Quantity sales. Special discounts are available on quantity purchases by corporations, associations, and others. For details, contact the publisher at the addresses above.   Orders by U.S. trade bookstores and wholesalers and Amazon Books.   Please contact Weirdvideos Distribution: Tel: (360) 421-7195; or visit www.Weirdvideos.com

Printed in the United States

DEDICATION

To my friend and professor,

Dr. George F. Howe
Master's College, Newhall, Ca.

CONTENTS

DESTINY OF MANKIND PERVERTED

What is being taught today as the Gospel and what is being evangelized "to the ends of the earth" is NOT the complete Glad Tidings ("well-message") of Great Joy brought by the angel for all men. Rather, it is a warped and distorted false teaching developed over many centuries of foul play by inconsiderate priestcraft.

It is understood by a minority of believers that a very clever deception has replaced the Good News. It is all good news until you reject it, thus, in the end, it is bad news! The gospel that is being spread is a double-tongued message. It is either a "let's make a deal with God" free-will gospel or an arbitrary and limited "pick-and-choose" to heaven or hell, without a choice, decision by God. In both cases, it is a "limited" salvation of man.

The glossing over and hence, the convoluting of the truth derives from an improper translating of God's Word. Whether by default and ignorance or by contrivance, the Greek Scriptures have been falsely interpreted to support a limited salvation. This distortion will be easily seen in the conflict and contradiction created between the traditional belief of Hell as everlasting and Jesus' teaching through the Apostle John, in the Book of Revelation, Chapter 20, verse 13 and 14 that it is "age-long" and lasts only up until the resurrection of the dead.

Such contradictions and false teachings derive directly from a poor understanding of Greek and Hebrew words. The following will show the reader how false translations can convert a word meaning into saying the exact opposite of what it originally meant, thus completely teaching the very opposite of God's true revelations.

The most important words in God's Scriptures are the little words eon and eonian. They either relay definite or undetermined time periods that have beginnings and ends or they refer to eternity. We shall see in the following discussions how these words have been contorted to make God's Word damn people forever, rather than remedially punish and correct them to bring them into the truth. We will see how Hell has been converted from the simple "unseen realm" of the Dead, into a place of everlasting misery for unsaved transgressors. We shall also see how this perversion of God's Word has made God out to "look" like a liar, a promise breaker. We shall also see that God warned us of this tendency in man to create and invent "another gospel", and how He incorporated failsafe messages in His Word to correct such devilish tamperings. Further reading to the end of this commentary will show the reader the uncovering and correcting of such errors, and the unveiling of the pure and simple Good News as handed down by the Prophets of old since the world began.

For a short synopsis of this book, see...

THE 76 WILLING'S OF GOD

1.   1Tim. 2:4 God will have all to be saved. (KJV) Can the will of God be thwarted?

2. 1 Tim. 2:5 God wills all to come to the knowledge of the truth. Does His will come to pass?

3. 1 Tim. 2:6 Salvation of all is testified in due time. Are we judging God before due time?

4. Jn. 12:47 Jesus came to save all. Will He succeed?

5. Eph. 1:11 God works all after the counsel of His will. Can your will overcome His?

6. Jn. 4:42 Jesus is Savior of the world. Can He be Savior of all without saving all?

7. 1Jn. 4:14 Jesus is Savior of the world. Why don't we believe it?

8. Jn. 12:32 Jesus will draw all mankind unto Himself. How does He do this if we only have an offer for this one life time?

9. Col. 1:16 By Him all were created. Will He lose a part of His creation?

10. Rom. 5:15-21 In Adam all condemned, in Christ all given live. Is this the same all?

11. 1Cor. 15:22 In Adam all die, in Christ all live. Again, is this the same all?

12. Eph. 1:10 All come into Him at the fullness of times. How many is all?

13. Phl. 2:9-11 Every tongue shall confess Jesus is Lord. Will the Holy Spirit fail to be given to everyone?

14. 1 Cor. 12:3 Cannot confess except by Holy Spirit. See what I mean? How many shall confess? See No. 13.

15. Rom. 11:26 All Israel will be saved. But most Jews don't believe yet!

16. Acts 3:20,21 Restitution of all. Does not mention any exclusions.

17. Lk. 2:10 Jesus will be joy to all people. Is there joy in an

eternal Hell?

18. Heb. 8:11,12 All will know God. How long, O Lord?

19. Eph. 2:7 His grace shown in the ages to come. Have we cut grace off where God has not?

20. Titus 2:11 Grace has appeared to all. Experientially or prophetically? A statement of promise to a future reality.

21. Rom. 8:19-21 Creation set at liberty. How much of creation?

22. Col. 1:20 All reconciled unto God. There's that word "all" again.

23. 1 Cor. 4:5 All will have praise of God. What for?

24. James 5:11 the End of the Lord is full of mercy. Is "hell" mercy?

25. Rev. 15:4 All nations worship when God's judgments are seen. Could His judgment be mercy?

26. Rom. 11:32 All subject to unbelief. Mercy on All?

27. Rom. 11:36 All out of, through, and into Him. All into Him? As ALL came out of, so ALL goes back in.

28. Eph. 4:10 Jesus will fill all things. Including an eternal hell?

29. Rev. 5:13 All creation seen praising God. No comments.

30. 1 Cor. 15:28 God will be all in all. What does that mean?

31. Rev. 21:4,5 No more tears, all things made new. "All" made new?

32. Jn. 5:25 All dead who hear will live. How many will hear?

33. Jn. 5:28 All in the grave will hear & come forth. How will the "righteous" Judge, judge?

34. 1 Cor. 3:15 All saved, so as by fire. How can fire save you as defined by tradition?

35. Mk. 9:49 Everyone shall be salted with fire. Including you?

36. Rom. 11:15 Reconciliation of the world. Will fire save the world instead of destroy it?

37. 2 Cor. 5:15 Jesus died for all. Did He died in vain?

38. Jn. 8:29 Jesus always does what pleases His Father. What pleases the Father? (1Tim. 2:4)

39. Heb. 1:2 Jesus is Heir of all things. Does "things" include people? Is Satan an heir to anything?

40. Jn. 3:35 All has been given into Jesus' hands. Can you accept this? How long does most of this stay in the hands of Satan?

41. Jn. 17:2 Jesus gives life to all that His Father gave Him. How many did the Father give Him?

42. Jn. 13:35 The Father gave Him all things. Study the word

"things" in the Greek.

43. 1 Tim. 4:9-11 Jesus is Savior of all! Can't seem to get away from that word "all."

44. Heb. 7:25 Jesus is able to save to the uttermost. How far is uttermost? To the extent of the whole universe?

45. 1 Cor. 15:26 Last enemy, death, is destroyed. Actually, it is the first THING destroyed!

46. Is. 46:10 God will do all His pleasure. Does the Old Testament agree with the New?

47. Gen. 18:18 All families of the earth will be blessed. Here comes that word "all" again.

48. Dan. 4:35 God's will done in heaven and on earth. What can defeat His will?

49. Ps. 66:3,4 Enemies will submit to God. Can any stay rebellious "forever"? Or, for "the eons"?

50. Ps. 90:3 God turns man to destruction, then says return. How can one return from "destruction" is defined as annihilation?

51. Is. 25:7 Will destroy veil spread over all nations. All nations?

52. Deut. 32:39 He kills and makes alive. Kills to bring life?

53. Ps 33:15 God fashions all hearts. "All" hearts, including men like "Hitler?"

54. Prov. 16:9 Man devises, God directs his steps What about "free will?"

55. Prov. 19:21 Man devises, but God's counsel stands. So much for "free will" and tradition.

56. Lam. 3:31,32 God will not cast off forever. Why does He cast off in the first place? (1 Cor 11)

57. Is. 2:2 All nations shall flow to the Lord's house. "All" nations?

58. Ps. 86:9 All nations will worship Him. "All" nations!

59. Is. 45:23 All descendants of Israel justified. Including the wicked ones?

60. Ps. 138:4 All kings will praise God. Are you catching on? Did you start out wicked?

61. Ps. 65:2-4 All flesh will come to God. That sounds wondrous.

62. Ps. 72:18 God only does wondrous things. I wish we would believe that.

63. Is 19:14,15 Egypt & Assyria will be restored. Really?

64. Ez. 16:55 Sodom will be restored to former estate. Sounds impossible.

65. Jer. 32:17 Nothing is too difficult for Him. Nothing? No, nothing! Not even reconciling ALL.

66. Ps. 22:27 All ends of the earth will turn to Him. For what purpose?

67. Ps. 22:27 All families will worship before Him. Praise His name!

68. Ps. 145:9 He is good to all. Including your worst enemies.

69. Ps. 145:9 His mercies are over all his works. Let's start believing that. Even the works He throws into Hades.

70. Ps. 145:14 He raises all who fall. Who hasn't fallen in SIN?

71. Ps. 145:10 All His works will praise Him. For "eternal torment?"

72. Is 25:6 Lord makes a feast for all people. And you are "willed" to be there.

73. Jer. 32:35 Never entered His mind to torture his children with fire. So, what is fire used for?

74. Jn. 6:44 No one can come to Him unless He draws them. You can't "chose" to follow Him. And you can't chose not to. See No. 75

75. Jn. 12:32 I will draw all mankind unto Myself Amen!

76. Ps. 135:6 God does what pleases Him. If it pleases Him to save all, are you upset?

NEW TESTAMENT USAGE
OF THE WORDS "eon" AND "eons"

In translating the Bible it is vitally necessary to be as consistent in the meaning of Greek words as possible. Mistakes can be made by accident, neglect, and ignorance in many cases. Yet, there is no excuse for translators to take extreme license to ADD, SUBTRACT or change God's Word in translation. But, thank God for His divine guidance that all these mistakes can be corrected.

The following will prove beyond a reasonable doubt that the words EON, EONS and EONIAN mean "Age", "Ages," and "Age-lasting" ("age-enduring"), and that these words are based on time-frames of limited durations, and that they DO NOT mean "unlimited" or "eternal" periods of time, such as 'eternity', 'eternal', 'everlasting', 'never-ending', or 'ever'.

The only way to translate the Scriptures and derive the truth is to be consistent with word meanings. The proper exegesis of a Greek word is to take every verse where the Greek word is used and study the context for the context will define the word. Among the many verses will be found definitive passages, ones that self define the word - these are stand alone verses that do not need any help. For example: "Before the great big 'X,' "after the big "X," or "at the consummation (Gr. "telos" END) of the big 'X'." Other passages will relay such ideas as "the big 'X' of all the X's," "the ONE 'X'," and "the many 'X's."

This tells us that the big "X" has a beginning and something before it and something after it, and that it cannot relay any idea of a "never ending big X" or "an on going big X." In other words, "the big X" cannot have an eternal, everlasting, never ending time value.

The best way to check the accuracy of this approach is to superimpose, without bias, the choices we have from a dictionary (lexicon) that list of meanings for "X", or in this case the word "EON". As to "eon" we are offered such ideas as, 1.) an immeasurable or infinite space of time; eternity. 2.) A long or short space of time; an age, a life span, a thousand years, seventy years, etc. 3.) The eons of geological time - a series of long ages. And 4.) (Gnostic Philos.) One of the embodiments of the divine attributes of the Eternal Being. Among the higher Æons are Mind, Reason, Power, Truth, and Life.

Notice now the complete contradictory meanings people have imposed upon this word in ancient as well as modern times: "age," "world," "eternal," "eternity," "forever," "ever," "ever-lasting," "never-ending." "Platonic year," "aeon," "age," "ages," "annus magnus," "century," "cycle," "cycle of indiction," "date," "day," "eternity," "generation," "great year," "indiction," "long," "long time," "long while," "month of Sundays," "right smart spell," "time," "years," and "years on end." Apparently, translators now have at their disposal a word they can use to say and mean anything they want.

When translating the Bible God has given His definition of His words and we must seek these definitions within the context of the Bible. It must be consistent, unless otherwise indicated. Needless to say, after some small effort, the student of Greek will find that there is only one consistent meaning (idea) for each Greek word and not two, three or more contrary meanings. hence, "up" does not mean "down" and "bad" does not mean "good." Moreover, Hell cannot captivate its occupants "forever," then un-captivate them at the resurrection! (Rev. 20:13).

Listing of all the Biblical verses that use the word eon will show the true meaning as "a period of time-period." It will be shown to always have a beginning and an end. Unlike older translations, which do not consider the Greek "tense" forms, the word EON can be both singular and plural, thus there are many EONS. Whereas, there is only ONE "eternity," one permanent "everlastingness," and a single "ever." Also, the word "eon" is a NOUN and not a verb!

Let us look at the word EON as an "age," which is consistently used by God Himself, will grantee a complete consistency in meaning throughout Scripture. There will be no inconsistencies, absurdities, contradictions, misunderstandings or ridiculous statements found anywhere in scripture using this meaning. Rather than invent alternative and contrary meanings in trying to make sense of Bible verses, and in preserving traditional dogmas, which make the word 'plastic', a consistent meaning leads us to a full understanding of God's Word as well as a correction of heretical teachings.

When the word "age" (a period of limited time) is compared to all other alternatives the twisting, bending, changing, and removal of Greek words by translators is becomes unnecessary. Obviously, using any other meaning other than "age-lasting" causes problems and confusion. The meaning that does not cause such errors should be the true meaning. Though, two or more English words are sometimes used to relay a true Greek meaning (idea), only one word is necessary in the case of the word eon. All other alternative meanings used to accommodate and support traditional doctrines and dogmas, such as a never ending Hell, will be shown to rake havoc within theology. Heretical doctrinal inventions imposed upon the Scriptures force translators to change God's word by adding, subtracting, and changing what does not accommodate their dogmas. It was done to "correct?" the Bible to say what the Greek text says otherwise. Study the following lists of word choices and decide for yourself.

The only consistent meaning for the words 'EON' and 'EONS' are the English "AGE" and "AGES". Even though the modern dictionaries define "aeonian" as 1.) Eternal, everlasting, lasting for an indefinitely long time, immortal, not subject to death, opposite of mortal. 2.) of or pertaining to an age. i.e. eonian, eternal, everlasting, immortal, lasting, etc., God has defined it differently. He has used it the way He wants to use it and has made it very plain in the Bible to mean "a period of limited duration."

The Nouns "AION" and "AIONS" or "EON" and "EONS" as used in Greek New Testament   should be best translated into the English equivalents of "AGE"   and "AGES". Using the English words AGE and AGES consistently throughout the text creates no problems. "AION" and "AIONS" when replaced with the words "WORLD" and "WORLDS" as alternatives appear to give some consistency with much less absurdity than using the other variants.

Yet, nevertheless it is less consistent than using "AGE(S)." The word "world," which is actually the Greek word "kosmo(s)" is not consistent with many passages when in conjunction with eonian when used in the same passage. It will be seen that it is inconsistent in many passages when used with the doublets "for-the" and "of-the." The passages make no sense, and some lead to complete contradictions when compared with other verses. See how the good translators of the King's Bible have translated "eons" in **Eph. 3:21,** then compare it with other verses that state *"the end of the world."*

EPH.3:21

(Gr.) doxa en tE ekklEsia en christO iEsou eis pasas
(Lit) glory in the ecclesia in   Christ Jesus into all
(KJV) glory in the church by Christ Jesus throughout all

tas   geneas   tou   aiOnos t On   aiOnOn
the generations of-the   eons   of-the   eons
 --   ages,   -- -- **world without end**

COMPARE WITH:

MATT. 13:49

(Gr)   houtOs estai   en   tE   sunteleia   tou   aiOnos...
(Lit)   thus it-shall-be in the   conclusion of-the eon...
(KJV) So shall it be   at   the   **end**   *of the*   **world...**

[Notice here that "*and*" would make no sense, so the translators correctly used "*of-the*" to translate "**tou**."]

Also, notice that **Gal. 1:4** can pass using "world" to translate "eon," but it cannot be used as a general rule of consistency. When "WORLD(S)" is doubled it sounds ridiculous and is meaningless: "WORLDS of-the WORLDS,"   "WORLDS and WORLDS" or "WORLDS of-the WORLDS." To avoid this the KJV translators used other words, such as "EVER," "forever," and "everlasting."

Using the verb "ever" in translating the noun 'EON' (age) creates a major problem for the translators, when in conjunction with the participle "THE".   So, taking license to force "eternity' into the translation, (thus an eternal Hell), they REMOVE the "THE" in over 50% of the Biblical passages! Notice that if consistently translated "ever" and "evers" as any good translator should, none of the passages make any sense, unless you remove the participle "the" from in front of it.   They had to SUBTRACT from God's Word to force the passages to support "for -- ever (and) ever."

HEB. 13:21

basanisthEsontai hEmeras kai nuktos   eis tous   aiOnas tOn   aiOnOn
being ordealized   of-day and of-night into the   eons of-the eons
tormented   day   and night   for   ever   and   ever.
                                                 (x)   (Gr. "*kai*")

[In this verse the use of "*of-the*" would not support the never endingness of torment, and so the translators used "*and*" instead, very well knowing that the Greek word for "and" is "*kai.*" Note as well that "*eis tous*" (into-the) had to be changed to "for." This is as bad as bad can get in mistranslating God's word.]

In the lists below we see that using "ever" in place of 'Age', "Ages" does give us some good passages conveying the idea of eternity, only if you are removing "the" from in front of the word. Yet, again when used consistently it creates horrible absurdities and contradictions. When it comes to such passages as conveying "this" ever or "that" specific 'ever' there are major problems. Matt. 12:32 "*...in this EVER*'. Notice Mark 10:30. "*...in the coming EVER.*" And Luke 20:34 is an even better example. "*...the sons of this EVER.*"

In using the word "FOREVER" we get no consistency at all and no meanings worth contemplating by even the most institutionalized of minds. See if you can find one passage that makes sense in the following usage of ETERNAL(S) as possible translations of EON(S). Remember CONSISTENCY must be the rule or we have chaos, and words begin to mean what God never meant them to mean.

Replace the Noun "AION" used in New Testament with "ETERNAL" and "ETERNALS" and you get the same nonsense. It is the same with using "ETERNITY" and "ETERNITYS". Try copying the EON list and substituting your own words and look to see if you can find any consistent word in English that will fit all the contexts EON(S) is used in. You may even try two combinations of English words "ooo-000" or maybe even three "ooo--000--xxx". You will see that the history of translating according to the minority, supports translating EON as "Age", a word having the meaning of a "certain-length-of-time" one with a beginning and an ending. The following altered lists of verses proves this.

Using the English words AGE and AGES consistently throughout the text creates no need to alter or change, add or subtract Greek words from the Scriptures. The complete consistency in using AGE and AGES shows us that there are NO problems in understanding God's Word. There is no need to violate the translation law of word consistency.

Replacing the words 'Eon' and 'Eons' with the word "WORLD" and its plural form "WORLDS" appears to give us some consistency with mush less absurdities than using other possible words, but it is nevertheless less consistent than using "AGE(S)". The word "world", which by the way is not "eon" but the Greek word "*cosmo*(s)" is not consistent with many passages when in conjunction with 'eonian' within the same passage. You will see that it is inconsistent and many passages make no sense when used with the phrase "FOR-THE". Some are beyond reasonable and lead to absurd statements. Notice that Gal. 1: verse 4 may well use the word World and even sound good to the ears, but it cannot be used as a rule of consistency when translating EON into English. The plural form or WORLD, when doubled up sounds absolutely ridiculous. It makes a muck out of God's Word. Of course, another word is used when dealing with these passages the word "ever".

[*   = Inconsistent, makes no sense when used in conjunction with phrase"for-the".   ** = Creates a contradiction; suggests a 'time before' or a 'time after'   an eon; a time period; age.]

If we follow the plural form of eon "eons" and translate 'world as a plural, "worlds", we get some real crazy translations. No wonder the Eternal Tormentors switched from one word to another and used "ever" instead. remember, the modern translations ALL remove the "the" and "for-the" from the translation process. Otherwise they would be forced to be more consistent and thus end in destroying their eternal hell fire lasting for "EVER".

Using the word "ever" in translating the word (noun) EON (age), creates a major problem for the translators, when in conjunction with the participle "THE".   So, taking license to force the nature of "eternity' into the translation, hence the eternality of Hell, they REMOVED it in over 50% of the contexts. Notice when properly consistently translated "ever" and "evers", none of the passages make sense - unless you remove "the" from in front of it. The same passages with 'THE' removed in translation to convey the eternal nature of things in the contexts.

In the above we see that using "ever" in place of 'Age', "Ages" does give us some good passages conveying the idea of eternity, only if you are removing "the" from in front. but when used consistently it creates again, horrible absurdities and contradictions. When it comes to such passages as conveying "this" ever or "that"   specific 'ever' there are major problems.   Matt. 12:32 "...in this EVER". Notice Mark 10:30.   "...in the coming EVER." And Luke 20: verse 34 is even worse. "...the sons of this EVER."

In using the word "FOREVER" we get no consistency in meanings worth contemplating. Not even the most institutionalized patients would dare try.

"THE DAY OF THE EON" is not the "now and forever." (2 Pet. 3: 18)

Orthodox translators habitually translate the Greek phrase "*doxa kai nun kai eis hEmeran aiOnos*" as "glory both now and for ever." This is not a proper translation of the Greek text in this verse. This translation glosses over the fact that the Greek is speaking of a particular day of a particular eon or "AGE." It speaks of some day at the end of a specific time and not a day within an eternity. To avoid exposing the word eon as an "age," the translators change the noun into a verb and superimpose the concept of everlasting, eternal and forever over the Greek, hiding the fact of ages to support agelessness. To admit that there are such things as ages and specific days that are important to God is to admit the corruption of many passages in support of eternal torment.   If translated properly, the verse supports the interpretation of eon as "age" and that there is a Day of Christ to take place at its end. To translate it as the Authorized Version does is to hide this day and extend "glory" beyond its culmination. The Greek text does teach   a culmination where glory reaches a end. Otherwise, though we may have a perpetual "glory," which sounds good, we have no "Day (into) of the Eon" where it becomes the Day of Jesus Christ.

The verse was never meant to say "Christ's glory "both now and for ever," or "Christ's glory for ever and ever." It says, "to Him be glory now, as well as into the Day of the eon." The literal translation says "Jesus Christ, to Him, the Glory, and Now and into (the) day of (the) eon. Amen." Comparing translations will reveal the error and the false doctrine of eon and eonian meaning "ever" and "forever."

sOtEros iEsou christou auto	hE doxa	kai	nun	kai	eis	hEmeran	aiOnos
amen. – Gr.							
Savior Jesus Christ to Him the glory and now and into Day of·eon,							
amen. – Lit.							
Savior, Jesus Christ. To Him [be] glory both now and for ever							
Amen. – AV							
Savior Jesus Christ. To Him *be* glory now, as well as into(for) (*the*) day of (*the*) eon.							
Amen! – CLV							

Other Supporting Passages:

"the day when[*] God will be judging the hidden *thing*s" (Rom. 2:16)

17

"in the day of our [*] Lord Jesus Christ." (1 Cor. 1:8)

"performing *it* until *the* day of Jesus Christ:" (Phil.1:6)

"no stumbling *block* ^{into}for *the* day of Christ," (Phil.1:10)
"into *the* day of Christ," (Phil. 2:16)

"that the day of the Lord is ^opresent" (2 Thess. 2:2)

ON THE WORD "eonian" AS "era-lasting", NOT "everlasting"

Friend.—I have taken the freedom to call upon you, to have a little discourse with you concerning the doctrine of the Restoration of all Things, which it is said you believe; and to propose some objections.

Minister.—1 am happy to see yon, and am willing to discourse, as well as I am able, upon any subject that may be agreeable; but 1 have always made it a rule never to press the belief of my sentiments upon my friends; and I can safely say, that, though such great pains have been taken by my adversaries, to prejudice people against me, I have never gone about from house to house to propagate my opinions; and I make it's universal rule not to introduce the subject in conversation, unless desired; but yet I never have refused to own my sentiments, when asked, respecting the matter; and am ready, in the fear of God, to answer any objections that can be made, to a doctrine which I believe is plainly revealed in the Scriptures of truth, and appears to me worthy of God.

Friend.—I shall first of all bring to view that grand objection, which is formed from the word eternal or everlasting, being applied to a future state of punishment; as in the following passages : Is. 33:14. "The sinners in Zion are afraid, fearfulness hath surprised the hypocrites. Who among us shall dwell with the devouring fire. Who among us shall dwell with everlasting burnings."

Dan. 12:2 "And many of them that sleep in the dust of the earth shall awake, some to everlasting life, and some to shame and everlasting contempt."

St. Matt, 18:8 "Wherefore, if thine hand or thy foot offend thee (or cause thee to offend) cut them off, and cast them from thee; it is better for thee to enter into life halt or maimed, rather than having two hands, or two feet, to be cast into everlasting fire."

St. Matt. 25:41 "Then shall he say also unto them on the left hand, depart from me, ye cursed, into everlasting fire prepared for

18

the devil and his angels." Verse 46. " These shall go away into everlasting punishment, but the righteous into life eternal or everlasting." The same word in the original being used for both, though varied by the translators. St. Mark. 3:29. " Rut he that shall blaspheme against the Holy Ghost, hath never forgiveness, but is in danger of eternal damnation.

2 Thess. 1:7,8,9 "The Lord Jesus shall be revealed from heaven with his mighty angels, in flaming fire, taking vengeance on them that know not God, and that obey not the gospel of our Lord Jesus Christ; who shall be punished with everlasting destruction from the presence of the Lord, and from the glory of his power."

Jude 6, 7 "And the Angels which kept not their first estate, but left their own habitation, he hath reserved in everlasting chains under darkness, unto the judgment of the great day : even as Sodom and Gomorrah, and the cities about them in like manner, giving themselves over unto fornication, and going after strange flesh, are set forth for an example, suffering the vengeance of eternal fire."

These texts, together, form such an objection to the doctrine of the Restoration, that I can by no means believe it, unless this can be fairly answered, and proofs brought fro>n the Scriptures to show, that the words everlasting and eternal, (which are translations of the same word and synonymous) being connected with the punishment of the wicked, and their future misery, do not necessarily imply the continuance of the same while God exists.

Minister.—I am glad that you have so fairly and fully stated the matter; and I highly commend your resolution, not to believe the universal doctrine, unless this can be answered fully, without any torturing or twisting the Scriptures; and if I am not able with God's assistance, to remove this difficulty, 1 will publicly recant my sentiments.

But, before I come to give a direct answer, I would beg leave to remark how very seldom this word is used to express the duration of punishment. We should think, by some sermons we hear, that everlasting is applied to misery in every book of the New Testament, if not in every chapter. A friend of mine told me, that he was once preaching in Maryland, and after sermon a man came and asked him of what denomination he was. To which lie answered, a Baptist. I think, says the man, that you do not preach up so much everlasting damnation as the Baptists and Methodists among us do. To which my friend replied, everlasting damnation is found in the Scripture.

True, answered the man; but some preachers give us more of it in one sermon than is to be found in the whole Bible. The truth of this remark will appear, if we consider that St. Luke never uses the word *aionion* or everlasting, as connected with the misery of the wicked, in his gospel; nor St. Mark hut once, and then in a particular case only.

In the gospel of St. John, it is not to be found at all in that connection, nor in any of his epistles: in the account of the preaching of the apostles through the world, in the first age of Christianity, we do not find it mentioned, in that light, so much as once: no, not in all the sermons, and parts of sermons, which St. Luke has preserved in the book of the Acts; though the doctrine of everlasting damnation is the substance of many modem discourses.

The Apostle Paul never mentions everlasting destruction bet once, though his writings form a considerable part of the New Testament. Neither ire such words found in the Epistle of St. James, or in those of St. Peter, and but three times in the Gospel of St. Matthew: and only twice in all the Old Testament. But was the word *aionion* applied to misery but once in the whole Bible, it would deserve a serious consideration; and unless the force of it can be removed by the authority of the Scriptures, it roast remain an unanswerable objection. But I shall proceed to answer it, by bringing. so equal number of passages where the word era-lasting is applied to things and times, that have had, or must have, an end. As in the following passages: Gen. 17:7,8. " And I will establish my covenant between me and thee, and thy seed after thee, in their generations, for an ever lasting covenant; to be a God unto thee, and to thy seed after thee. And I will give unto thee, and to thy seed after thee, the land wherein thou art a stranger, all the land of Canaan, for an everlasting possession; and I will be their God." Verse 13. "He that is born in thy house, and bought with thy money, must needs be circumcised : and my covenant shall be in your flesh for an everlasting covenant."

Here note that the land of Canaan is called an everlasting possession; and the covenant of circumcision in the flesh, an everlasting covenant, though it is certain that the land of Canaan, as well as the other parts of the earth most be dissolved or melted, in the general conflagration;" and circumcision is now declared null and void by the Holy Ghost; and the ceremony cannot endure to endless ages. Of the same kind are the following passages: Gen. 48:3,4. "And Jacob said onto Joseph, God almighty appeared to me at Luz, in the land of Canaan, and blessed me: and said unto me, behold, I will make thee fruitful, and multiply thee, and will make of thee a multitude of people; and will give this land to thy seed after thee, for an everlasting possession." And in the blessing of Joseph he says, "The blessings of thy father have prevailed above the blessings of my progenitors, unto the utmost bound of the everlasting hills." By which, I suppose, the hills of the land of Canaan were meant.

God saith to Moses, Ex. 40:15. "And then shalt anoint them (Aaron's sons) as thou didst anoint their father, that they may minister unto me in the priest's office; for their anointing shall surely be an everlasting priesthood, throughout their generations." Lev. 16:34. "*And this shall be an everlasting statute onto you, to make an atonement for the children of Israel for all their sins, once a year; and he did as Jehovah commanded Moses.*" The apostle declares, that these everlasting ordinances were only till the time of Reformation, Heb. is. 10, and this everlasting priesthood of Aaron's eon, had ceased long ago: "For the priesthood being changed (by Christ there is, of necessity a change also of the law for he of whom these things are spoken pertaineth to another tribe, of whom no man gave attendance at the altar: for it is evident Ihat our Lord sprang out of Judah ; of which tribe Moses spake nothing concerning priesthood. And it is yet far more evident, for that, after the similitude of Melchisedek, there ariseth another priest, who is made not after the law of a carnal commandment, but after the power of an endless life: for he testified] that, thou art a priest forever, after the order of Melchisedek : for there is verily a disannulling of the commandment going before for the weakness and unprofitableness thereof." Heb. vii. 12, 18. The whole sum of the apostle's argument, in this epistle, tends to prove that the everlasting ordinance is now no more ; and the everlasting priesthood of Aaron and his sons is now abolished.

Another passage where the word everlasting is evidently used in a limited sense, is Numb. 25:11,12,13, where we read thus: "Phinehas, the son of Eleazer, the son of Aaron the priest, hath turned my wrath away from the children of Israel while he was zealous for my sake among them, that I consumed not the children of Israel in my jealousy. Wherefore say, behold, I give unto him my covenant of peace: and he shall have it, and his seed after him, even the covenant of an everlasting priesthood : because he was zealous for his God, and made an atonement for the children of Israel."

If the word everlasting intends endless duration, how shall we be able to reconcile this promise with the total cessation of the

21

Levitical Priesthood ? As for the family of Phinehas, with whom this covenant of an everlasting priesthood was made, it was entirely deprived of the benefit of the same, within the space of four hundred years; for when the sons of Eli transgressed the covenant, by profaning it, God sent him word, that as they had broken it on their parts, it was entirely, and to all intents and purposes, dissolved. Read 1 Sam. ii. from the beginning of the 12th verse to the end of the 17th, and from the 27th to the end of the chapter: and also, chap. 3: 11,12,13, 14,

I will transcribe verse 30, of the second chapter in proof of my point. " Wherefore Jehovah, God of Israel, saith, I said indeed, that thy house, and the house of thy father should walk before me for ever: but now Jehovah saith, be it far from me, for them that honor me, I will honor; and they that despise me. shall be lightly esteemed." Hophini, and Phinehas, were soon after slain in one day; and Saul the King of Israel, sent Doag the Edomite, who fell upon the priests and slew fourscore and five persons, who wore a linen ephod, in one day. " And Nob, the city of the priests, smote he with the edge of the sword; both men, and women, and children, and sucklings, and 'oxen, and asses, and sheep, with the edge of the sword." 1 Sam. 22:19. The whole house of Phinehas seems to have been destroyed at this time except Abiather; and when Solomon came to the throne he thrust him out from being priest, "that he might fulfill the word of Jehovah, •which he spake concerning the house of Eli, in Shiloh," 1 Kings 2:27. From this time the house of Ithamar had the priesthood.

It is so evident that the word which is translated everlasting, cannot in the nature of things, absolutely signify, without end, that 1 should not think it worth while to quote any more passages in proof of its intending age or ages, only, were it not constantly used as a great objection against the universal Restoration; 1 shall, therefore, instance two or three more in particular in this place, and refer to a great number of others, of the same kind ; all tending to prove the same thing (Heb. 3:6). "The everlasting mountains were scattered, the perpetual hills did bow.'* The gospel is called " The everlasting gospel," Lev. 14:6, yet it must cease to be preached, when it shall be needed no longer. Jonah saith, "The earth with her bars was about me forever; yet hast thou brought up my life from corruption; O Jehovah, my God." Jonah ii. 6. But it would be the highest absurdity upon the supposition that the word here rendered forever, properly signifies without end, for him to say, that his life was brought up from corruption; and, therefore, we know that he could not use it in that sense, because, on the third day, he was delivered from his dreadful prison. There is no doubt but the time that he was there, seemed an age, and, while he was thus shut up, there was no intermission to the darkness, and distress that overwhelmed him; and, therefore he might say, with propriety, that earth, with her bars was about him, forever (i. e. perpetually without cessation) during the period he remained in the fish's belly ; which appeared to him, as a long age indeed. But, as it would be a work of much time and labor to mention all the passages where the word translated forever, evidently intends only an age, or period, I shall just direct you to the following; which you may look over at your leisure.

Gen. 13:15. 43:9. 44:3-2.—Ex. 12:14, 17, 24. 21:6. 27:21. 28:43. 29:9, 28. 30:21. 31:16, 17. 32:13.—Lev. 3:17. 4:13,18, 20,22. 7:34, 36. 10:9,15, 16:29, 31. 23:14,21,31, 41. 24:3. 25:30, 46.—Numb. 10:8. 15:15. 18:8, 19. 19:10.—Deut. 4:40. 15:17. 18:5, 28, 46.—Josh. 4:7. 14:9.—1 Sam. 2:30. 3:13. 27:12. 28:2.—1 Kings, 12:7.—2 Kings, 5:27.—2 Chronicles, 10:7.

ETERNAL TORMENT
PERVERSION OF THE SCRIPTURES
A WARNING!
Corrupting the Scriptures
and
Perverting the Promise of God

"I testify to everyone who hears the words of the prophecy of this book: If anyone adds to them, God will add to him the plagues which are written in this book; and if anyone takes away from the words of the book of this prophecy, God shall take away his part from the tree of life and from the holy city, which are written in this book" (Rev. 22:18-19. NAS).

"You shall not add to the word which I am commanding you, nor take away from it" (Deut. 4:2. NAS).

ADDING and SUBTRACTING words from the Bible has unfortunately been done from Genesis to Revelation and has brought more than 1500 years of sorrows upon the world (Rev. 22:18). The definitions of many Greek words have been construed and twisted to mean the complete opposite of what they originally meant. It is mostly done by following incorrect lexicons and dictionaries and not by accurately studying the contexts. Furthermore, translators push to favor the creed, rather than the context.

The distortion of God's Word leads to the perversion of the Promise of "the Restoration of all," and therefore, to a hopeless future for many. It is the "left behind" and "left out" hopeless humanity that makes people question God's integrity. It is very important how we translate the Bible. It can mean the difference between life and death.

It is permissible to paraphrase the Bible for easy reading and to state such is the case. But to change the translation of the manuscripts, construe them to say what they don't mean, or mean what they don't say, and then seal it with a false stamp of infallibility libels one to the harsh judgments mentioned in the above verse 18. Publishers should clarify what translations should be used for easy reading and for establishing doctrine. Doctrine must not be the by-product of superficial paraphrases.

Traditional religion has apparently adopted an erred view of the final state of man and completely obliterated the truth of the reconciliation of all. Most churches today continue to follow these flawed translations resulting in the calamitous situation we see in our religious institutions today. There is no question that the majority of the problems that plague the churches today originate from the errors of poor translations.

The results of proper translating are clearly different from the usual traditional Latin and English renderings. For example, translators have made it appear that the smoke of "*the great city Babylon*" (Rev. 18:10, 19:3) rises up "*for ever and ever*" and not "*for the Ages of the Ages.*" With the end of the human Kosmos and the beginning of the judgment of men's works, we know that the physical smoke of any city would come to an end.

Notice in the following how words have been removed and others added, while still others are changed. The changes in meaning are obtained by transforming nouns into verbs. What this verse means in the original language is that the smoke goes up for a period of time, or for "the ages of the ages." In the revised (corrupted) translation, interpreters have mistranslated it to mean, the smoke goes up eternally and never stops. It is "for ever and ever." This poor translating of words corrupts many other verses as we shall see.

Rev. 19:3

autEs anabaninei	eis	tous	aiOnas	tOn aiOnOn.
ascending	into	the	eons	of-the eons.(CLV)
ascending	into	the	ages	of-the ages.(YNG)
rose-up	for	--	ever	[and] ever. (KJV)

The proper translation is...
"And her smoke rose up into /throughout/ the eons of the eons."

The changing of "tous aiOnas tOn aiOnOn" into "*for ever and ever*" has been done 46 times throughout the whole Bible. It has been done (coincidentally?) 13 times in the Book of Revelation! This is surely a sinister number and reveals through divine numerology the fouling of meanings in God's Revelation! [This may be true to some extent, since Francis Beacon, an Illuminist during the reign of King James, was part of the translation of the 1611 Bible and most assuredly knew full well what the words meant. They apparently 'purposely' disregarded the true meaning.

26

In the following examples, translators have purposely removed the Greek word "*tous*" (Eng. "the"). They have replaced the Greek word "*ton*" (English: "of-the") with the grammatical conjunction "*kai*" (English: "and"). Whereas, they knew full well the proper translation of these words in all other passages, for whenever there is no denoting times and ages, they properly translate "ton", "tous" and "kai".

One of the simplist of Greek words is "kai" and it is well known to not be a replacement for "ton" or "tous". The Greek word kai is not even present in the specific verses using "*tous aiOnas tOn aiOnOn*". Any Greek student knows this and it does not take a PhD to see what has been done.

By adding, subtracting, and changing Greek words, both ancient and modern translators have changed God's prophecy. What was originally meant (according to the biblical context) to be for the AGES alone, has been extended into "eternity." For example, the consequence is what was once an age-lasting remedial punishment (judgment) is now transformed into an eternally tormenting damnation. This poor translation fouls up each and every verse that uses "*tous aiOnas tOn aiOnOn.*" For a complete list of every verse using this phrase, see the last portion of this book.

The contemporary prophetic view of the future is false. The ultimate and final reconciled destiny of the lost is converted into "eternal separation." Consequently, the majority of people are eternally damned and Christ is made to fail in His mission to draw all towards Himself. He appears to not be the heir to all things but only inherits a small portion. Christ is still the Alpha (beginning) of ALL, but He is no more the Omega (Heir) of ALL. It was all created FOR him, but most of it will be lost and He is only the heir to whatever is left of creation.

The hellfire and damnation pulpit pontiffs ignorantly prophecy and quack that most WILL go to Hell "FOR EVER AND EVER", and with no escape. Yet, Christ says, He will call forth all the dead from out of the hell, from the heavens, from the sea, and from the earth to the judgment of men's works (Jn. 5:24-25, Phil. 2"10 and Rev. 20:13).

The above perversion glosses over the fact that the "ALL" confessing Christ as Lord shall consist of all humans that have ever lived. This is shown by comparing the following verses:

Jn. 12:32 "...*shall be drawing all to Myself.*" We must ask: Drawing all of what? The Greek says "all," but the Authorized Version (KJV), exposes the limitation fraud, by clarifying all as "all men." They add the word [men] in brackets.

Phil. 2:10 "*...every knee should be bowing, celestial, and terrestrial, and subterranean.*" This verse covers every creature made by God, as to those who have a brain for reasoning and the ability to confess. Their "every" (willing and reasoning) tongue shall be confessing" (Phil. 2:11). The verse leaves no intelligent creature out.

The things "in heaven", "above earth", and "under the earth" are all of God's heavenly (intelligent) creatures. The onus of the Bible centers upon the whole human race everywhere - believers in heaven, men in (on) earth and the dead under the earth in the unseen realm - hell. It looks like God is clearly saying that "all" (all that is sinful - humans) shall hear His voice and come forth "confessing."

Contemporary theology is contrary to Biblical truth. God's judgment and wrath are only for "the ages of the ages"(Young's Literal Translation) and NOT "for ever and ever" as many think. Rather than most being damned, as tradition teaches, all people are remedially corrected and then purified (Gk. "pur" fire) by Christ, after being "drawn" toward His final reconciliation of all. The contemporary majority assertion concerning this promise is false.

According to Bible prophecy, traditionalists and dogmatists preach and teach a destiny that is not true! One may well assert that "many" go to Hell (the Grave, the "Unseen Realm"), but it is the amount of time in Hell that is at issue. This question has all to do with what Christ actually did on the Cross! To say anything other than what is really promised is to make Jesus fall short of His intentions.

To make changes to this critical area of judgment is to degrade the atonement, malign God's loving character and literally hack Christ's work. It is false to preach and teach the eternal damnation of souls, when God is preaching and teaching the reconciling of the whole human cosmos. It simply amounts to a big change with one small word. A jot and tittle changed can mean the difference between God eternally cursing or remedially correcting His creations. It can mean the difference between God being the "heir to all" He created or losing.

In Revelation 9:3, (and I am not making this up nor being judgmental) the Lord Himself is referring to a Great Prostitute that corrupts the whole earth with her theological lies, changing the WORD OF GOD to support her false teachings. Unfortunately, the Latinists are responsible for the corrupt Latin translations of the

Greek as well as the last 1800 (plus) years of the dark-age. The consequences of changing the little word "eon" to mean "eternity" creates a limited atonement and a limited salvation of humans. The germans, the Englishmen, and many others did an equal job in mistranslating the Latin and Greek into our modern versions.

One may wonder exactly what the Devil would do to poison the whole earth with a false message. Obviously, God did not allow him to touch the Greek and Hebrew to make the Bible. When it comes to lexicons, dictionaries and "translations" there is no such divine protection. Obviously, God authored the original monographs, but the Devil translated most of them into what we have today. We may wonder if the ancients were really all that ignorant of Greek? This language is fairly simple and is known to be a living language and not a dead one. There is no reason other than perpetrated fraud in the mistranslation of Scriptures.

Now, as to the smoke of the great city of Babylon, does this smoke actually ascend up "for ever and ever," or does it only rise up "into the Ages of the Ages?" This is absolutely relevant to the destiny of lost souls, when it comes to damming people forever or judging them only for the ages. This difference has all to do with a proper view of God's love, mercy, justice, and truth.

We shall resolve this mistake and set the account straight, as to what happens to all people after the resurrection of the dead, especially those who do not know Jesus.

ET CORRUPT TRANSLATIONS

Let us first establish a Biblical truth and principle held by the majority. The Bible does not contradict itself. God would not give us a salvation message that teaches two opposing truths. This would neutralize any message from being understood and create mass disinterest. The interpretation and understanding of the truth depends on the context and what time period or "age" is being discussed. Otherwise, it becomes muddled and the application of truth becomes confused.

A GOOD example, illustrating the violation of the above is the horrible teaching of the eternal damnation of people. Comparing the following verses will expose the blatant falsity of such a teaching. A proper translation of the texts will bring a correction of the error and an exposure of the true destiny of humanity.

First of all, it must be understood that EON and eons (plural) never once, in any context, relays the meaning or eternity, eternal or forever. Every passage that uses these words demands the meaning of "age" and "ages" or some undetermined but limited period of time. Sometimes this time period refers to a determined amount of time, such as in the life span of a human: "seventy years." Thus, rather than eternities and eternities, God is shown, after "AGES and AGES" have passed, to lift His indignation on all Israel (Rom. 11:26 "all Israel shall be saved"), as well as all non-Israelites (2 Chron. 20:6, Ps. 102:15, Ex. 39:23, Am. 9:12, Ob 1:15, and especially Gal. 3:8).

OLAM AND EON

To establish the truth, one must compare the Old Testament Hebrew "Olam," with the Greek word "Eon," and the English equivalent, "Age". With this understood, we shall see what happens when we insert the meaning "everlasting" in into some important Biblical verses dealing with prophecy and future things.

Obviously, one will notice that Jeremiah is transformed into a false Prophet! Furthermore, to explain this problem, the churchmen have incorrectly supposed the prophecy is "conditional."

JEREMIAH'S PREDICTION
SAID TO BE EVERLASTING
(JER. 17:1, 27 and 23:39, 40.)

17:1 *"The sin of Judah [is] written with a pen of iron, [and] with the point of a diamond: [it is] graven upon the table of their heart, and upon the horns of your altars;"*

17:27 "But if ye will not harken unto me to hallow the sabbath day, and not to bear a burden, even entering in at the gates of Jerusalem on the sabbath day, then will I kindle a fire in the gates thereof, and it shall devour the palaces of Jerusalem, and it shall NOT BE QUENCHED."

23:39 "Therefore, behold, I, even I, will utterly forget you, and I will forsake you, and the city that I gave you and your fathers, [and cast you] out of my presence:"

23:40 "And I will bring an everlasting reproach upon you, and a perpetual shame, which shall not be forgotten." -- (KJV)

YET,
THE PROPHECY IS NOT EVERLASTING!
(JER. 30:9, 22; 32:42.)

30:9 *"But they shall serve the LORD their God, and David their king, whom I will raise up unto them."*

30:22 *"And ye shall be my people, and I will be your God."*

32:42 *"For thus saith the LORD; Like as I have brought all this great evil upon this people, so will I bring upon them all the good that I have promised them."* - (KJV)

So, which is it? Is God holding the sin against Israel "forever" or is He holding it on them for a certain period of time – such as, for "an age?" Does God reconcile them or not? Let us compare a few more verses to verify this purposely obscured truth.

HELL IS NOT "EVERLASTING"

First, HELL is said to be "eternal" or "Everlasting," yet we find this is contrary to what Rev. 20:13 teaches.

Notice in this passage that death and Hell (Hades) give up the Dead rather than captivate them "forever."

Even though hell has an unquenchable burning aspect (Mark. 9:43, 45), that could be used by God to destroy the body, soul and spirit (Matt. 10:28), and it appears that there is no escape from it (Matt. 23:33) for the wicked and all the nations that forget God, nevertheless, Ps. 9:17, Mark 9:43, 45, and Matthew 10:28; 23:33 say that the people "which were in them" do "escape" (See also Ps.9:17, Ps.16: 10 and Prov.23:14).

So, how long do people stay in hell? For eternity or for some "age-long" period?

THE DEAD RELEASED FROM HELL
(Rev. 20:13)

"...and death and Hell delivered up the dead which were in them..."

What a contradiction we have! Which is it? Is Hell everlasting ("for __ ever and __ ever") or is it for for a period of "limited" time, for "*the Ages of the Ages?"* As Revelation 20, verse 13-14 says, departed souls go there "for the Ages of the Ages", and then death and hell are emptied. After this vacating death and hell are abolished or put to no more use.

How can we extort from scripture that people stay in Hell forever, then read later that it is emptied of its captives and abolished? The translators falsely insert the word "and", replacing the true Greek words "of the."

The designated length of existence for the Lake of Fire is ALSO based on the same set of Greek words "ages of the ages", establishing the true and proper TIME-FRAME duration. It is the same set of words! It cannot mean temporary one minute, then eternal the next.

Rev. 20:10
basanisthEsontai hEmeras kai nuktos eis tous aiOnas [tOn] aiOnOn"
"and shall be tormented day and night *for --------ever [and] -- ever.*
(KJV)
"shall be being ordealized day and night *into the **eons** [of the] **eons**."*
(CLV)

The Lake of Pur (Fire) only lasts "for the AGES of the AGES." Then, it too comes to an end. It was created beforehand for the Devil and his angels, and it will be abolished when it is of no use anymore.

Consequently, eternal torment, which is not supported by the Greek time-frame of "ages of the ages" is a misunderstanding. Annihilation, which is also not supported by the CONTEXT is also a false interpretation. This leaves only one other alternative: Universal Reconciliation. The LOGIC dictates this and the Greek Supports it. The context supports this "ages of the ages" limited time period with no contradictions created in any other passages using the expression.

KING JAMES SAYS "the" EQUALS "and"!

Many translators falsely reinterpret the Greek phrase "of-the" as meaning "and." Thus, Hell and the Lake of Fire are designated as being "eternal" or "everlasting," rather than understood as a limited amount of time. The length of existence for both is based on the same set of Greek words, which establishing the true and proper TIME-FRAME for both events. It is the same set of words" "for the ages of the ages." In other words, these places lasts only "for all the ages, of all the ages, which exist" and no more.

Look closely at the passages and how they have been corrupted.

[AV = King James Version and most all other English translations;
CLV = the Concordant Literal Version, by Concordant Publishing
Concern; YNG = Young's translation.]

Rev. 20:10

hEmeras	*kai*	*nuktos*	*eis tous*	*aiOnas*	*tOn*	*aiOnOn* (Grk)
of-day	and	night	for the	eons	of-the	eons (TRNS)
day	and	night	for -	ever	**(and)**	ever. (KJV)
day	and	night	into the	eons	of the	eons." (CLV)

The above verse proves Hell to last only for "the AGES of the
AGES." It comes to an end when Christ calls all the dead to rise up
out of it. Therefore, eternal torment is not supported by the Greek
expression "eons of the eons." The annihilation of souls is not
supported by the context either. This leaves only one other
alternative and that is Universal Reconciliation. If we cannot
"eternally torment" the dead or "annihilate" them, then we must ask
what happens to them.

The Greek text supports the truth of limited punishment, and
logic dictates the same, because the context defines it. With this
translation corrected, there are no contradictions in all the other
passages that use the same expression "for the eons of the eons."
This expression of limited duration is the most consistent
translation with the most perfect understanding. There are no
contradictions.

One mistake modern translators make is disregarding the
determiner "the" in front of nouns "eon" and "eons." They also
disregard the word's singular and plural forms. In fact, they
purposely translate them as adverbs! The word "ever" is an adverb
and the translators know this. How is it that they take a noun to be
an adverb? Adverbs do not have prefixed participles.

THE removes AND is added

Jn. 6:58 [--- = removed]

trogon	*touton*	*ton*	*arton*	*zesetai*	*eis ton aiona* GK
one-chewing	this	the	bread	shall-be-living	into the eon (trans)
masticating	this	---	bread	shall be living	for the age (CLV)
eateth of	this	---	bread	shall live	for --- ever (KJV)

Notice in this verse the translators leave out "ton" (Eng. "the") from in front of the noun **aiona** (Gk. "eon"), magically transforming it into an adverb, "ever." The word *aiona* is also in the singular tense form.

Heb. 7:24

"But this [man], because he <u>continueth ever,</u> hath an unchangeable priesthood." (AV, KJV)

Well, personally I cannot make any sense out of the above translation. Maybe there is a problem with the word "ever"? Let us translate it properly and then see what it says.

ho de dia	*to*	*menein*	*auton*	*eis*	*ton*	*aiona*	GK
he yet thru	the	to-be-remaining	Him	into	the	eon	TRNS
yet that one,	because of His remaining	into	the	age	CLV
But this [man],	because he continueth	x	x	ever	KJV

Now, let us see this section in context of the whole verse.
*"And these indeed, are more than one, having become priests because death prevents them from abiding; yet that One, because of His **remaining (into)for the age**, has an inviolate (perfect, unprofaned) priesthood"* (Heb. 7:23-24).

In the above the Authorized Version leaves out TWO words, completely REMOVING the words "into" and "the," which converts the noun eon into an adverb. It forgets to add the word *eis* "into" or "for."

In some cases it is just, for English grammar, to leave off the determiner "the" because it is a known "given thing" that the word is being used as a noun. In most cases, "the" is used to point forward to a following qualifying or defining clause or phrase, and because it sounds better and helps to distinguish nouns. But when a determiner is removed to specifically transform a noun into an adverb, where the text uses it as a noun, it is a perpetrated corruption!

Both ancient and modern translators purposely leave out the Greek word eis ("into") to purposely destroy the concept of "remaining into" or "throughout" something. By removing the word "into," or "for" they make the verse say that God Himself continues forever, rather than in "not continuing into something" that only lasts for a particular length of time.

Translators could have easily used the other word "always" as they have done in Heb. 7:25, but for reasons unknown, they do not. Nevertheless, one thing is knowable, there is absolutely no justification for removing these words other than for glossing over the understanding of "age-lasting."

IF "eon" WERE TO MEAN "ever" OR "forever"

Oute   en touto to aioni   oute   en   to   mellonti   (GK)
Neither in this the eon   nor   in   the ***one***-impending.   (TR)
Neither in this   -   eon   nor in ***that which is*** impending. (CLV)
            this   AGE   (YNG)
Neither in this   - world, neither in the *(**world**)* to come.   (KJV)
*Neither in this   - EVER,   nor   in the **EVER**   to come.*

Interpretation:
"Neither in this AGE, nor in the Age which is impending."

In the above passage, the AV translates the Greek word ***aioni*** ("eon" - singular for one AGE period) into "world," which is a based on a completely different Greek word. In other verses translators use the word "ever." In this passage, they disregard the fact that "world" or "system" in Greek is ***kosmon*** or ***kosmou***. [See Matt. 13:22] Yet, in **Matt. 13:35** the translators revert back to using "world" in translating kosmou. So, does ***aioni*** mean "world," "system," "ever" or "age?"

Consistency demands that it means a specific AGE or period of time. If the dogmatic translators are to be consistent, it would be translated *"Neither in this - EVER, nor in (the) EVER to come."* But, they knew, as well as we do, that the expression "the EVER" makes no sense. So, to avoid such nonsense, and to cover up the true meaning of an age-long period, which would expose the "eternal" or "forever" nonsense, the Divine etymologists force the (only other optional replacement term) "world" (kosmon) into the passage. It is obvious that they DO NOT WANT to use the consistent meaning of "eon" (age), because this would expose to the reader that the translators knew "ever" and "forever" had beginnings and endings. This becomes more apparent when it comes to the contradiction of the world ending and not ending.

DOES THE WORLD END OR NOT?

The reason most translators confuse the words eon, age, ever, everlasting and world (system) is either because of ignorance or to hide the true meaning of aioni (age). Watch what happens with the following two famous contradictory verses.

Notice also that when the proper meaning is re-inserted, the verses are perfectly in sync and do not contradict each other. In Matt. 13:38 the AV translators properly use the word "world" to translate the Greek word kosmos, which means system. So, we know that they knew what kosmos meant. Yet, in the very next verse, they distort the passage (that coincidently uses aioni) by using the word again. Verse 39 uses aioni to describe a period of time (an age) that is to come to an end.

To hide the fact that an eon has an ending, the AV transposes the word "world" over the Greek aioni. It is very apparent why they use the word "world" and not the word "ever." The word "ever" in not universally consistent. The passage would not make any sense. For example: "*the harvest is the end of the EVER.*"

To avoid being forced to expose an eon as an age-lasting period, they stuff the word WORLD in its place. This disallows anyone from seeing the proper understanding: "the harvest is the end of the AGE" or "the harvest is the conclusion of the eon."

Furthermore, by doing this, while having no other choice, they make the "world" have an end, whereas we see below that the world does not have an end. Well, maybe it does and we cannot know one way or the other, unless we understand the verses with their proper meaning.

According to traditional rules it should be translated: "*throughout all ages, for ever and ever*" or "*throughout all generations, for ever and ever.*" *But, this smacks of making the generations of mankind last "for ever and ever" rather than come to an end. No matter, with such a poor translation, and Hell bent desire to cover up "eon" as an age period, they cannot help but relay that the generations last in "world without end."*

First, we see that the AV translates geneas as "ages" and not properly as "generations." The Greek uses eon for an age and eons for ages. Next, all of the determiners "the" are removed. The word aionos is again mistranslated as "world," while the next few aionon (ages) are purposely construed to mean END!

Matt. 13:38

ho	de	agros	estin	ho	kosmos	GK
The	yet	field	is	the	system (world)	TRNS
Now, the		field	is	the	world	CLV

And,

Matt. 13:39

hu	de	thorismos		sunteleia	tou	aionos	GK
the	yet	harvest		conclusioin	of-the	eon	CLV
the		harvest is the	end		of the	world	AV

Is. 45:17

u·la	thklmu		od	·oulmi	od ·p	Hebr.

And·not   you shall·be·confounded unto eons·of future TRNS
They shall not be ashamed/confounded for   future eons CLV

MOST FAMOUS FOULED UP VERSE!

Eph. 3:21

eis	pasas	tas	geneas	tou	aionos	ton	aionon	GK
into	all	the	generations	of-the	eon	of-the	eons	TRNS
for	all	the	generations	of the	eon	of the	eons	CLV
throughout all		ages,				world without end		KJV

Besides this, we are to swallow another miracle with the Greek word "ton" (which means "of-the") as transubstantiated into "without". So, just how in God's will do they derive "without" from this Greek passage? (See above in Eph. 45:17). So far, we have been swallowing for over 2000 years the idea that "ton" can mean OF-THE, AND, as well as WITHOUT, and even be removed without consequences!

Also, aionon (eons) is erroneously pawned off to mean END, whereas in almost every other Bible passage, it is falsely translate as "ever" and "everlasting." It is not that they are trying to make true sense. Rather, they are trying to cover up the truth. This railroading of Scriptures to support the traditional dogma that judgment and hell is "forever" is no accident!

So far, we can see that the traditional translators have purposely distorted and mistranslated the words aionos and aionon - "eon" and "eons" - to mean what they need them to mean: i.e., "world," "age," "end," "ending," "ever," "forever," and "everlasting" as long as they can avoid the "age-lasting" concept.

The translators of our English Bibles did a very poor job in translating the Greek word "aion." It occurs a little over 100 times in the Greek New Testament. In our King James Version it is translated 'world' 32 times, 'for ever' 27 times, 'for ever and ever' 20 times, and by a few other words some-times. Only two times out of a little over 100 is it properly translated 'age' (Eph. 2:7; Col 1:26). Two out of a hundred is a very poor record.

The King James is not the only Bible that invents multiple meanings for eon. In most of our English Bibles eon is given 40 different renderings: Age, eon, time, period, today, the future, universe, course, world, worldly, world without end, since the world began, from the beginning of the world, ever, evermore, for ever and ever, end of my days, eternal, everlasting, always, permanently, constantly, of old, ancient times, all time (since) time was, (since) time began, (before) time began, all time, (since) the beginning of time, eternal ages, eternal life, eternity, course of eternity, utter (darkness), (the son) does (remain), ages of the eternities, (in and through) the eternities of the eternities, etc.

The word 'aionios" is equally miraculous in meaning anything:- everlasting, eternal, eonian, age-lasting, age-during, age-duringly, age-abiding, (in) the time of the ages, age-times, (before) the ages of time, of the ages, (in) the periods of past ages, (before) the ages began, for the ages of time, (before) the beginning of time, since the world began, (before) the times of the world, (before) times eternal, from eternity, from all eternity, for ever, unfailing, final, unending, permanent, immemorial, enduring, lasting, eternally, long, perpetual, an immeasurable eternity, last, heavenly.

Nevertheless, their tampering and tinkering with God's written word has exposed their dogmatism. They only hope that people do not read nor question the contradiction of the world ending in one passage and not ending in another passage.

Furthermore, no matter if questions are raised, they have done a good job covering up the true meaning of eon. Consequently, Hell, death, and judgment are not seen as temporary, corrective, and remedial measures of God, but rather as everlasting torment - God forbid, if men were to find out that translators buried the truth of "the Promise of the Restoration of All" (Acts 3:21).

What this conspiracy of mistranslating is covering up is the reconciliation of all mankind and the renewing of all creation. The alternative consequence would be the abolition of the phony "eternal torment" doctrine.

HELL IS TEMPORARY

One of the few interpretive passages on the subject of Hell is **Revelation 20:13-14.** The passage, when properly translated exposes the errors of traditional orthodoxy. Rather than injecting a fear of a vindictive God of "eternal" wrath and "everlasting" Hell, it comforts the listener with a vindicating God, judging human works with restorative measures.

Some verses may seem to suggest a vengeful God when using words such as "destroy", yet God has made it clear that Hell is an "Age-Lasting" place of limited duration that apparently leads to restoration. Furthermore, the meaning of destroy is "ruin." Our concept of destroy is ceasing to be. Whereas, the Greek text means "to ruin," "ruination" or "to tare-down and weaken."

"And the sea gave up the dead which were in it; and death and HELL delivered up the dead which were in them: and they were judged every man according to their works." [KJV]

Apparently, the Greek text teaches that HELL lasts only so long as God's wrath and that His wrath does not abide forever. Thus, an everlasting HELL cannot be part of God's glad tidings of great joy for all the people. Most of orthodoxy, if not all of it, unfortunately for many, is teaching the very opposite - that Hell does NOT give up its dead.

What is seen in the traditions of today is a false gospel intruding into Christian truth, the very one that the Apostle Paul warned about. It is the *"Jesus is gonna save me, but not others"* limited atonement gospel. It is, alternately, the Electionists understanding *"Jesus only died for the limited elect, because it is only applied to a limited few, and therefore, Jesus only died for 'some' and not all."*

Well, the truth is, Jesus loves you and is your personal Savior, and this is very true, but it is NOT true that He is not the Savior of all others as well. He is actually the Savior of all mankind, even though He is especially (but not exclusively) the Savior of those who believe. Just because people do not believe now, and because people do die not believing, does not necessarily mean that they will "never" come to believe.

The ALPHA and OMEGA of GOD

Jesus said, through St. John, that He is the "Alpha and the Omega, the beginning and the end" (Rev. 1:8, 11, 21:6 and 22:13). What does this actually mean and what is the significance of this title? Let us analyze the Greek text to see what we can find as to the meaning.

We will see that this title houses God's creation beginning, the first prophecy of the "restoration of all" and the prophecy's fulfillment at the end of the ages with ALL tongues confessing, and the reconciliation of all mankind. This includes the culmination and drawing in of all [created things] into the ownership and hands of God. We shall also see that every eon, every human event, and every doctrinal truth flowing in-between this Alpha and the Omega does point, on the human time-line, in support this truth of total restoration of all that God created.

This title establishes, if one has the eyes to see, the foundation of universal restoration, which does establishes the reality of universal salvation. We shall also see that this "restoration" not only "saves" many from being dumped into the garbage heap, but also "salvages" those that have.

The Greek text records this "Alpha and Omega" principle in Revelation, Chapters 1, verses 8 and 11, 21 verse 6, and 22 verse 13...

In these verses (below), we see that Jesus is the Alpha or origin, "the beginning." The word Alpha is the first letter in the Greek alphabet, which is a word derived from it. The root word of "alphabet" is alpha. He also said He is the Omega or "finish," the "telos", which means "consummation." In verse 1:11, He terms Himself as "*ho eschatos*" (the last). The Greek meaning of "*prOtos*" (first) is "BEFORE-most." In being the prOtos "Before-most", Christ must be the "AFTER-most" when He says He is the "telos" or consummation of all things.

Verses 1:8 and 22:13

egO	eimi	to	ha		kai	to	O	archE	kai	telos
I	am	the	Alpha	and		the	Omega	Origin(al)	and	Finish

(consummation)

1:11

egO	eimi	to	ha		kai	to	hO	ho	prOtos	kai	ho	eschatos
I	am	the	Alpha	and	the	Omega		the	First	and	the	Last

(Before-most)

21·6

egO	eimi	to	ha	kai	to	O	hE	archE	kai	to	telos
I	am	the	Alpha	and	the	Omega		the	Origin(al)	and	the Finis

(beginning) (consummation)

In the above verses, we see that Jesus is the Alpha or origin, "the beginning." The word Alpha is the first letter in the Greek alphabet, which is a word derived from it. The root word of "alphabet" is alpha. He also said He is the Omega or "finish," the "telos", which means "consummation." In verse 1:11, He terms Himself as "***ho eschatos*** " (the last). The Greek meaning of "***prOtos***" (first) is "BEFORE-most." In being the prOtos "Before-most", Christ must be the "AFTER-most" when He says He is the "telos" or consummation of all things.

If He is going to be the Before-most, He must also be the After-most. It appears that the word "most" here is in reference to Himself being the "fore-most" of all things created, and actually the "BEFORE-all." So, therefore, if we are willing enough to understand, it is not hard to see Christ as the "before-most," the "fore-most," and the "after-most." It is not detracting, but supportive to say, that He is the "Before-all," the "for-all," and the "after-all." This fits perfectly with Him being the "Creator of all," the "Savior of all," and the "Heir to all."

Now, a question derives from the above symbolism. What was Christ before this Alpha beginning? The Bible gives us the answer. Jesus is the One that was before the Creation. Christ was the foremost, the first, the beginning or creator of all the Cosmos, and everything that is in it, whether it be in the heavens, on earth, and whether visible or invisible, as well as thrones, dominions, principalities and powers (Col. 1:16).

St Paul understood this, just as we should understand, that "by Him were all things created" (Col. 1:16), and thus, we may further understand, that "by Him all things consist" (Col. 1:17). In being the Before-most, Christ is the One that brought everything (created) into existence.

Now, as the creator of everything, Christ must also be the owner of everything and not just in the past, but of all that is at present and all that is to in the future (end). For He said, that He was the "telos," - the Consummation.

The word *telos* is not only a word used to denote some end or "event horizon," but is the most significant title name of Jesus Christ Himself. Jesus said "I am the telos" or "the consummation," and not just the cause of it. This of course, in light of the fact He IS "the BEGINNING" makes Him the finishing End result or *eschtos* of all things.

As the title of the movies series "FINAL DESTINATION" demonstrates, the final end result of people is death. But, Christ is claiming here that He IS the FINAL DESTINATION of all things, and nothing will escape Him as the "telos" or finality and the Owner of all. To be the maker of all in the past, and the Owner of all in the present, He must be the Heir to all in the future. All things were created by Him, and through Him (Rom. 11:36), because all things were created FOR Him (Col. 1:16)

Needless to say, but say it we will, all "things" (including all people, Jn. 1:7) will be reconciled to Him (Col. 1:20), because God "sent not His Son into the world to *condemn* [any part of] *the world*, but that the [whole] world through Him might be saved" from God's wrath (Jn. 3:17 and **Rom. 5:9**). This this context of Bible synonyms, the word "might" is synonymous to "will."

Job is ever so true, when he said that "The soul of every living thing, and the breath of all mankind is in His hand" (Job 12:10). Job is speaking in the present tense. And it makes sense to say that if Christ is the Beginning, and the End, He must also be the Middle as well. If He is the First letter of the alphabet, and the last letter of the alphabet, he must by necessity be all the middle alphabetical letters.

So, if we understand that Christ was before and IS the before, and that all came from His hand, and that all is in His hand now (according to Job) then, as He IS also the "After-all," and the actual consummation itself, we can easily understand that, as "the finality" or telos of all, every created thing must end up in His hands. He IS the consummation of all Creation, and He resides in Heaven presently until the time of the restoration of all, which God spoke through the mouth of His holy prophets, throughout the ages (Acts

3:21). This is the Glad Tidings "Well-message" of the Biblical Universalist prophets today.

If we may play on words, we can say that Christ is the "Foremost" now, because He was the Before-most in the past, and because He will be the After-most in the end. God, After-all, will be the All in all that "filleth all in all" things (Eph. 1:23), after everything is subjected to Him (1 Cor. 15:28).

Now, though there are diversities of opinions upon this subject, most even denying this truth, "*it is the same God which worketh all in all*" (1 Cor. 12:6), both the good and the bad, the truth and the falsities, and even making all stubborn, so that He may have mercy upon all (Rom. 11:32), to fulfill the promise of the Restoration of All.

"*Jesus Christ is the faithful witness, and the first begotten of the dead, and the prince of the kings of the earth. Unto Him that loved all humanity, and washed everyone's sins in His own blood, and is making us kings and priests unto God and his Father; to Him be all glory and all dominion throughout the ages of the ages. Behold, Christ is coming with clouds; and all the eyes of humanity shall see Him, even they that pierced Him: and all the kindred of the earth shall wail because of Him...*" (Rev. 1:5-7).

"*Behold, the tabernacle of God is with humanity, and He will dwell with everyone of them, and they shall be His people, and God Himself shall be with all humankind, and be their God. And He shall wipe away all tears from their eyes; and there shall be no more death, neither sorrow, nor crying, neither shall there be any more pain: For the former things [earthly mortality] are passed away. For Christ said, 'Behold, I make all created things new.' And Jesus said unto me [St. John], 'Write: for **these words are true and faithful.**'*" (Rev. 21:3-5).

CHRIST: Son of GOD and HEIR TO ALL that was Created.

"*God, who at sundry times and in divers manners spake in time past unto the fathers, by the prophets, Hath in these last days spoken unto us [all humans] by [his] Son, whom he hath appointed Heir of ALL [things], by whom also he made the worlds; Who being the brightness of [his] glory, and the express image of his person, and upholding all things by the word of his power, when he had by himself purged our sins, sat down on the right hand of the Majesty on high,*" (Heb. 1:1-3) (["things"] is not in the Greek Text).

44

COMMENTARY:

The OMEGA, "telos" consummation (end result), in the "restoration of all" the creation [as the prophecy says], must be equal in the positive [good], to the ALPHA "beginning" or creation. For, the ALL was created by Him, for His pleasure"

Thus, the end result must be equally pleasurable to Him and therefore, as "THE ALL is subjected under Him," God may be, "the ALL in all."

The following verses are extremely clear that we (who believe) are to understand that Christ is not just the propitiatory sacrifice for our sins only (those that believe in this age and life), but is equally the same "applicable" and "effectual" propitiation for the SIN of the entire world. The entire world are all those others, whom many believe are not saved, and will not be saved, because they cannot be saved, or because they will not believe, or those that God does not (wills not?) to choose and saved.

"But, he is the propitiation for our sins: and not for ours only, but also for [the sins of] the whole world" (1 Jn. 2:2).

It is also necessary to mention that, God is surly the One... "Who is willing ["thelei"] ALL ["pantas"] humans to be saved and to be coming into a realization of the truth" (1 Tim. 2:4).

THIS IS NOT A WISH, DESIRE, HOPE or some other questionable feeling of "chances are, most will not make it," but a plain statement of FACT, that ALL will be reconciled without question.

And this is what WILL BE TESTIFIED TO IN DUE TIME. As it is written: "For, when we were yet without strength (yet sinners), in due time Christ died for [ALL] the ungodly" (Rom.5:6). "Who gave himself [as the] corresponding ransom over all, to be testified in due time" (1 Tim. 2:6).

ALL DELIVERED FROM HELL'S FLAMES

"Our [all men's] God, whom we [believers] serve [because Christ served God for us all] is [more than] able to deliver us [all humans] from the burning fiery furnace [Hell], and He WILL deliver us [all humans] out of thine hand, O king [Satan]" (Dan. 3:17).

In this New Dispensation of pure grace, no man is better than another in the eyes of God. Christ has covered all in His Blood atonement. In the old dispensation, men stood alone. But in this new one, Christ stands in all our stead. He represents us all to the Father, whom is well pleased, not so much with each of us, but with His son.

Christ is our ransom and he paid it for all humanity, especially [understood by] those who are believing. As these men were delivered from the king's flames, so every man shall be delivered from the devil's flames, for Christ defeated the works of this devil.

One work of the devil is to have all men burn for eternity. As it is with false doctrine, the devil will have most, but not all. As to God, He wills that all men be saved and come to the knowledge of this truth. This is not the gospel from Hell, as many believe, but the truth from heaven - "His will be done on earth, as it is in Heaven."

Christ has truly taken all the captives captive and delivered all mankind from Hell's eternal captivation. Though, many will say, "To Hell with this. This teaching is a doctrine of the devil. Turn the heat up more. Let them burn forever!" (Dan. 3:19), rather, the Lord says, "Hell will be no more," and He says this through St. John's Revelation, Chapter 20, verse 13. These words are true and faithful! *"And the sea gave up the dead which were in it; and death and Hell delivered up the dead which were in them; and they were judged every man according to their works."*

HELL, THE LAKE OF FIRE, AND DAMNATION ARE NOT "EVERLASTING"! FOR, GOD PROMISES "THE RESTITUTION OF ALL"

After Adam and Eve's transgression (SIN), God made a promise to them and their children that He would reconcile all back to Himself; that He would ultimately reverse all that the Serpent influentially caused. This promise was handed down by prophets of pre-flood times, who taught the "restitution of all."

Noah and his family brought this "promise" over on the Ark and hand it down through Shem, who (as Melchezedic) then hands it over to Abraham!

1.) God reaffirms this promise to Abraham, who is to be a blessing to all the nations of the earth, all kindred, and all peoples in his "seed", which is Jesus Christ. This is a direct and blatant statement of the universal reconciliation of all mankind. For, this promise was based on the previous promise made before Abraham was born to the people of Adam, and that was the prophecy of "the restitution of all peoples and creation." As shown above, this was handed down by the Prophets, since the age of the Fall of Man began or "since the world began" as the King James translation says.

2.) This promise was handed down by God through His specially chosen people "Israel" and to be remembered through the Mosaic sacrificial system. The Priest's sacrifice was to be made for the the whole House of Israel, to foreshadow the promise that ALL Israel will one day be saved. Yahweh accepted this SINGLE sacrifice as an "atonement" for all Israelites, not just a few that just so happened to personally believe and be devoted to the sacrifice.

3.) To fulfill this promise and seal the future destiny of all mankind, God the Father sent His Son Jesus Christ to fulfill the whole law of Moses. The law of Moses incorporated certain laws of atonement - the atoning for all the SIN of Israel - of all Israelites.

The Apostle Paul teaches that God now, in the Church Age, includes all the Gentiles in this salvation plan and not just racial Israel, for their is now no more racial differences between Greeks, Jews, and all other races. Thus, the Good News of this universal atonement is to be preached to not just to Jews only, but to all the Gentiles as well, and to all creatures - hence to all mankind!

4.) According to the design and definition of Moses' sacrifice, Christ's sacrifice must also "cover" or "shelter" all of Israel, but now all the Gentiles as well - i.e. all mankind. Since, the Mosaic sacrifice was an applicable atonement that literally covered (forgave) all the sin of Israel, and was not just an offer to those who should be accepting it, and sense Christ's sacrifice was to be definitively based upon the Mosaic, His sacrifice was meant to cover or shelter all Israel and all the gentiles - all human beings, from birth to death, and beyond death, even to those who have died in the past.

5.) Based on the above references, the definition of the atonement of Jesus Christ was and is a universal atonement for all mankind, literally and applicably, and is that true light (Law) every man is born with, whether he is aware of it or not.

6.) That this generally applied atonement and specifically applied "salvation" are two aspects of a grand restitution plan by God to reconcile all mankind and creation, and are references to two working aspects: First is the sole "work" of Christ in atoning for all mankind to reverse what Adam did 100%. Thus, the atonement is applied to everyone that will ever be born; and this is qualified by St. John who speaks of the "light" that every man is born with; and it is without any human choice.

Christ's atonement is that guarantee or the force behind the "drawing" or "dragging" of all promised in His raising from the dead that secures the ultimate confession of all tongues, and the bending of all knees of all mankind at the great culmination of all things.

Whereas, the second work, "salvation" is that aspect of the atonement, which designates that a human being has become enlightened or "saved" from the darkness of unbelief, and thus reborn into an awareness of this universally applied atonement.

The first "guarantees" all mankind an ultimate restitution back to God, which is the ultimate destiny of humanity. This is the sole work of Christ, whom is the heir to ALL - and this is the choice of God and not of any man.

The second aspect ("salvation") is the new birth from out of darkness and judgment into salvation, and into an awareness of being atoned for by Christ. This is a partial responsibility of man and is surly obtained by grace through faith; for by grace, through faith is one saved: And faith comes by hearing, and hearing by the word of God, and only by a preacher from whom this gospel is heard. This believing, and consequentially. the Sealing of the Holy Spirit inwardly, secures the believer as to his immediate destiny, and this is in regards to his passing on into death to be immediately with Christ. For those who do not believe yet, they pass on into the grave, death, Sheol, Hades or as some translations say, "Hell."

7.) Yet, Hell and the Lake of Fire are not eternal places of permanent damnation and non-correcting torments, but are "time-based," "eonian" or "age-lasting" temporary (unseen realm) remedial places of correction, reconciliation and cleansing through punishments and purification. For, after Hell's fury (base on a designated time period - and for that matter, also the Lake of Fire), Hell ceases to be of use and it is emptied of all it's captive occupants (in the resurrection of the dead) into the judgment of man's works. At this point, the righteous continue in the presence of Christ, while the unrighteous proceed through PUR-ification in the Divine Lake of PUR - or Fire, which even so, just as Hell, comes to an end, also lasting only "for the eons of the eons," at which time it also empties all it's captive occupants into the final "restitution of all" at the end of the ages.

8.) After all is said and done in man's Cosmos, and at the end of the Ages (eons), and at the great culmination or restitution of all, everything and everyone will be subjected to God the Father, that He may be the ALL in all. Everyone ever born will confess with their tongues and believe in their hearts in Jesus Christ, for they will have no excuses, and neither will they have any desire to have any excuses. Every eye shall see Him for who He really is and what He has really done, and shall be glad to believe - for "seeing at this time is believing. Everything, which was created, shall also be reconciled back to God, which was originally created by Christ, through Christ and FOR Christ, who is the sole "heir" to all.

9.) Finally, and truthfully, it must be understood that Satan is not an HEIR to anything God created: No material substances or intelligent living entities - not one human being is to be forever separated from God, nor be captive or the everlasting property of the Devil.

No one and no thing is to belong to him forever and be eternally separated from God. Just the idea of "separation" of God suggests that God is not omnipresent, whether spiritually geographical or outside of His creations.

The Lake of Fire is no more eternal or everlasting than Hell. This flushes eternal torment down the sink and leaves annihilation of souls as the theologians only theological recourse against Universal Reconciliation. But the truth comes to the forefront that HELL ('grave', 'Sheol', 'the pit', 'prison', 'the unseen realm') and the Lake of Fire do not annihilate their occupants! Annihilation is not supported in Scripture. It is not taught by God in His Word.

If we turn to Revelation we see that God brings many souls out of death and Hell, the Sea, the places under the earth, on the earth and those in the heavens, to stand before Him. From this point, there are many souls found fallen short. A large group is marked with the Beast. And, yes, these folk are tossed into the burning lake.

The Book of Life is then opened. Many are found not written in the Book of Life. Many souls are thrown into this Lake of Fire, "*where there is already the Beast and False Prophet.*" Now notice that the Lake of Fire contains "the Beast and the False Prophet." They are NOT annihilated, nor are they said to be in a process of being annihilated. They are there suffering torments, "day and night, for the eons of the eons." where their "worm [spirit?] never die, nor is the fire quenched" (as long as they are there). Now, how long are they there for? And, after this, is the fire quenched? Yes.

These souls are there being "be tormented day and night" for "the EONS of-the EONS" only, and not any longer. All these EONS come to an end and thus this Lake of Fire comes to an end. This is what many believe is the beginning of the so called never-ending

49

final state. The last option left can only be for the RELEASE of the occupants from the Lake of Fire to be reconciled, since they are not eternally tortured nor annihilated.

This is the reconciliation of those not yet saved, as the only third and final position to take. The culmination of all and the reconciliation of all, after all judgment is over, finally removes the last consequences of the curse on Adam Mankind - mans grieving and resisting the Holy Spirit. Since death has been abolished and Hell (the grave) has been put to no use, God's irresistible grace eventually draws all to confession and acknowledgment of Christ as the Son of God.

All areas of where the dead were are now empty. No one is being 'eternally tormented', no one has been annihilated. So, everything that was ever created stands at the threshold of this Great Beginning of Bliss, the redemption of ALL, with full knowledge of the Son of God, Jesus Christ. ALL has now become as it was meant to be and all creatures have bowed their heads, and bent their knees, and ALL Creation is reconciled. Jesus has subjected Himself to the Father, and His Kingdom has been subjected to the Father so that His Father can now be the ALL in ALL.

THE GREEK WORD "PUROS" MEANS FIRE

The Greek word for fire is "*puros*", the root word to our English word 'purify'. 'The Lake of Puros' is a place where fire is used to smelt out impurities. To purify something is to 'fire-ify' or to put to the Smith's furnace, whatever needs impurities removed, such as the 'sin' in this analogy of tormenting souls. The subject is not to annihilate the object, but to hammer out or torment "extract" the sin nature that dwells in them. God is that Great ALL consuming Fire. He is the one who, in His wrath, tortures out ALL that is corrupted in man, to bring ALL His Creation into perfect purity and unity. As He was the Fire in the Burning Bush in front of Moses, so He is this Fire that saves souls, "so as by fire."

The reason that Hell and death appear to last "for ever and ever" with it's associated never ending burning fire of punitive damnation and torment, is because of the translation of "for ever and ever" is a mistranslation [interpretation] off of the Greek phrasing "for the eons of the eons" or "for the ages of the ages."

The problem is not very apparent, unless one looks at a

comparison between the English interpretations and the Greek manuscripts. Let us compare this to see the obvious mistakes. Let us compare the verses and the translations and see what has been changed. Let us look at the words "eternity", "forever","everlasting", and "ever" and see that the translators knew very well that if they fiddled with these words enough, they could pawn off upon the public the eternal torment doctrine. Here are the various ways EON is used in the Greek Bible.

GREEK VARIANTS relating to the "for the AGES of the AGES". [i.e. KJV: "for ever and ever".]

1.) "for-the eons of-the eons" = [plural + plural]
2.) "into-the eons of-the eons" = [plural + plural]
3.) "for-the eon of-the eons". = [singular + plural]
4.) "for the eon" [singular]
5) "for-the eons of-the eons, and beyond" = [plural + plural + Ages end + Great Beyond starts].

TIME DESIGNATIONS in relationship to the Words EON, EONS and EONIAN (Age, Ages, and Age-lasting).

An EON can...
1.) be future   = Mark 10:30
2.) have a beginning   = Eph.3:9 and Luke 1:55
3.) have an end!   = 1 Cor. 10:11 and   Heb. 9:26
4.) be chained together into a long series of Eons, which have an end   = Eph. 3:21

Now, look at some poor translations using the word "eternity" as a replacement word for these variations of eon as used in the Greek text and how it malfunctions as a usable word replacement, when compared with other verses that use the same Greek word.

REVELATION 20:10
Etymology Breakdown and Comparison between the Greek and English.

hmeras kai	nuktos,	eis tous	aiwnas	twn	aiwnas	GR
of-day and	night,	into the	EONS	of-the	EONS.	TRNS
.of-day and	night,	for the	AGES	of the	AGES.	CLV
		through-out-the)	AGES	of the	AGES	
day and	night,	for x	ever (and)	xx	ever.	KJV

[Should be   = |____for the____ever __(of the) ever.

x ="the" is removed

xx – "of-the" removed and changed to "and"

After about the sixth century after Christ the Latin Church had completed her mission in totally fostering the false teaching that Hell was an eternal place of no return. Almost everyone but a few small groups was forced under her hateful measures of torture and threats of burning in Hell, to believe it as a universal truth. Before this, most Christians believed in the universal restoration of all mankind.

The Lake of Fire became a permanent vacation resort for the Damned, because the Church also taught that a person has only ONE CHANCE here to believe or burn. All further forgiveness is denied once they enter Hell, especially the Lake of Fire.

To support this position they had to alter Greek word meanings and they did this by altering the meanings in the translations. They did not touch the Greek manuscripts because very few people had access to them, if any at all. So from Greek it went into the Latin language that Rome maintained, then later as Latin faded away as a language, it was converted into German and Old English, especially in the reformation period.   By this time all the errors were pretty much crystallized in the minds and translations of the day. Originally, the Greek told us it was only "for the EONS" or ages. Now, after a few thousand years, they have brainwashed people to read and believe it is now "for EVER and EVER." But, God does not allow HIS WORD to go misunderstood for very long - there is an age that He decides to put an end to the rubbish being taught.

The message was clear in what God was saying, yet they choose to change it for personal gain. Only the Devil would deceive a soul to pervert the true meanings, where that soul could care less about the consequences! It was a contrived perversion of Scripture by wolves in sheep clothing, that Jesus and Paul warned us about. They would enter into the body and bring in falsehoods, heresy, lies and other foreign traditions of men, and they could do this by contorting the scriptures to teach and justify such teachings. And they would do this in full comfort that God would not do anything to stop them or punish them. They might not have even believed there was a God. All this was done with NO FEARS of the warning in Revelation 22:18-19.

The Translators did the very thing God told them NOT to do. They were warned to not ADD to, SUBTRACT from or change this Book. But they did not listen, nor did they care. They had an agenda to pervert God's message to put people under fear and control them: "God will damn you to eternal Hell if you do not eat this communion wafer!"

They ADDED the word "and" where there was none to replace the little phrase "of-the", and changed the word EON into the word "ever"; the root of our word 'everlasting'.

They SUBTRACTED the word "THE" and left it out all together changing the meaning of age to 'eternity'.   The word EON is a noun, just like the word 'BIRD' is a noun, because we use the word THE in front of it. "A" and "THE" designate nouns such as in "a bird" and "the bird". The Greeks did the same thing to designate a noun. Our modern translations, all favoring and following this tradition of the older translations are filled with these toxic corruptions, because the translators ADDED, SUBTRACTED and CHANGED God's Revelations.

Compare these verses between the Greek and the English and see how they twist a word to mean two different things:

Here we see that the AV (KJV) version out right changes the word eon "aiwni" to 'world' which is really the Greek word Cosmos. It is most interesting that the translators took the root word 'eon' and changed it to "world" when they knew very well that it was based on the word "eonian", which means 'age-lasting', or as they would have us believe, 'everlasting'.

en tw kairw toutw kai en tw 'aiwni' tw ercomenw zwhn aiwnion
Transliteration:
in the season this and in the 'eon'   the   coming   life   eonian
Translation:
in this era, and in the coming Age,   life age-lasting.
Distortion:
in this present time, and in the 'world'   to come life everlasting.
                    (should be KJV, "ever")

53

How one can get "world" out of the word "ever" or "ever-lasting" is beyond my understanding. It appears that they would have us believe that the Greek words *eon* and *eonian* have multiple and varied meanings, even contradictory meanings: There is "ever", "everlasting" and "world," and in some passages "age"! Here are some more interesting mistranslations that expose this perpetrated fraud.

mustEriou *chronois* aiOniois sesigEmenou
of-close-keep (to)-times eonian having-been-hushed
of-[the]-secret having been hushed (to/in) age-lasting
                                                    [past]-times
of the secret hushed in age-lasting past times
which was kept secret since the world began (KJV)

The above King James Translation is horrible! If the translators were true and consistent to their understanding of the word eonian, we should be reading it as one of the following:

"...which was hushed up, since (the) everlasting began."
Or "...which was hushed up, since (the) ever began."
Or "...which was hushed up, since (the) forever began."
Or "...which was hushed up, since (the) eternity began."

Here we have the secret kept, but not the rest of the truth in the passage! Now, why didn't they translate 'eonian' here into "everlasting" like they do in most other passages? It is because the context would not allow them to do so. The passage dictates a period of time or times in the past when such mysteries were hushed up.

It openly demonstrates that 'eonian' is referring to a series of past eons or ages, when the secret was kept hushed up, but, now the mystery is brought to light. So, eonian has a meaning of a limited time period. The only way to avoid the dictates of the context was to completely give 'eonian' a whole new meaning - such as WORLD.

Sense the World had a beginning, and could have an ending, whereas an "everlasting" or a "forever" could not, the only recourse to get a limited timing inserted into this passage, without exposing eon as "age-lasting" was to alter the word by replacing EON with some other limited period - cosmos, and use the limitations of the planet Earth - so the word "WORLD" was forced into the passage.rather than using age or eon - which is supposed to always be "everlasting."

There is just no way "ETERNITY" could be stuffed into this passage and be pawned off onto the readers without exposing their fraud. Here are the changes they made, to make things simple: EONIAN, rather then meaning "everlasting" or "age-lasting", now means "WORLD". CHRONIOS, rather than meaning IN-TIMES (past tense in this case), now means "SINCE-BEGAN". HAVING BEEN HUSHED (past tense), now means, "WHICH WAS KEPT".

Another passage that gave the translators their Hell, but would expose them to ridicule if they did not do something, is Titus 1:2.

ep	elpidi	zOEs	aiOniou	hEn	epEggeilato	ho
on	expectation	of-life	_eonian_	which	promises	the

in expectation of age-lasting life, which God, who does not lie,

In hope of ETERNAL life, which God, that cannot lie,

apseudEs	theos	pro	chronOn	aiOniOn.
un-false	God	before	times	_eonian_.
(the one not lying)	before			_the ages_
	promised	before	age-lasting	times.
	promised	before	_the WORLD began._ (KJV)	

How do translators get around the fact that an eon or a "times eonian" is a time limited period, and that an EON has a beginning? Again, "times eonian" has been changed into WORLD because "everlasting" and "forever" does not work nor would it make any sense.

Watch in the first case that they translate eonian into "everlasting", but in the second case they use the word WORLD instead. Why? Because, in the first case the translators can get away with using "everlasting" as a substitute English word without exposure. The second case, forces them to use another term, sense that one has a time period or age that came before it.

The above verse should be translated as such, according to their rules of word meanings, if they were consistent with using the translation "eternal".

"In hope of ETERNAL life, which God, that cannot lie, promised before the ETERNAL began."

Unlike no other word in human language, we now have at least one word; 'eonian' translated into two completely non-cognates words. 1.) ETERNITY, and 2.) WORLD.

Again, we see that whenever the word 'eonian' is used in context with a time designating word such as "before" (GK. 'pro'), the translators had to use some other term other than ETERNAL. If the word ETERNAL would have been used, it would have a time period coming before it. They just cannot have "BEFORE (the) ETERNAL" or, "BEFORE ETERNITY," because it would not make any sense. But, using the expression "BEFORE (the) WORLD" would do just fine - that is, if no one knew the difference between the Greek words EONIAN and KOSMOS. And, they would not since they were Latin speaking readers.

Sense the common people at that time knew very little about Greek, switching eonian with cosmos would not be noticed. The word WORLD, which had a beginning, and thus could have an ending, would deceive the reader and hide the fact of the real meaning of "eonian". It would allow the perversion of the first 'eonian" to be changed to "eternal" without being noticed.

Look at Ephesians 3:21 as another example, but not the least at all, in the ADDING, SUBTRACTING and changing of God's Word by our Latin and English translators.

christO	iEsou	eis	pasas	tas	geneas	tou
Anointed	Jesus	into	all	the	generations	of-the
Christ	Jesus	throughout	all	-----	ages,	(KJV)
aiOnos	tOn	aiOnOn	amEn			
EON	of-the	EONS,	AMEN.			
world	-without?	end	men. (KJV)			

Perpetrated forgery! Blatant false translation! The Divines, Scribes and Pharisees above say, that the world has no end, while they must agree that other verses say it does not. So which is it? World without end, or a the world has an end? Read the following...

1 Cor. 10:11
"upon whom the ends of the world (age) are come."
Heb. 9:26
"but now once in the end of the world (age) ...to put away sin."
Eph. 3:21
world **without end**   Amen.   (KJV)

The Kings English translators more than obviously committed the Revelation 22:18-19 transgression error in their ADDING words that are not in the Greek; SUBTRACTING words that were there and removing the determiner "the". They also changed the Greek word "OF-THE" into "AND."

This sounds complicated, but it is very simple once you see it in print. This changed a lot of meanings in Scriptures to bring in the teaching that Hell and the Lake of Damnation were everlasting places, equal to the everlastingness of Heaven.

First, the KJV folk very well knew what the Greek word "AND" was. It was the little word *kai.* But they preferred to deceive their readers by manipulating it the way they wanted to support eternal damnation.

They also knew what the Greek word "OF-THE" was, and that it was *twn.* Again, they twisted this one to mean something else for a particular purpose. They also knew without a doubt what the Greek was for "INTO-THE" and "FOR-THE." This is the little phrase *eis-tous.* But, this little truth also caused them problems, so they contorted it as well to fit the agenda of promoting eternal suffering.

We do not want to get into why the translators did not see or care to use the PLURAL and SINGULAR forms of the word EON. Maybe they did not know the tense forms. We want to start out first with seeing that the words 'for-the' and 'into-the' and 'of-the' have had the THE removed from the passage. This they knew darn well was not the right thing to do, nor that it was not good and acceptable in the sight of God.

This would leave us with the words 'into', 'of' and 'for' left behind to be used in the passages. This changes the noun 'EON' [AGE] into the perversions 'ever', 'forever' and 'eternity'.   Without this change it would have left them with "for THE-ever" or "for the eternity", and "for the eternity and the eternity"., which infers and suggests that there are more than one 'ever', 'everlasting', and 'eternities'.

Now, let us see how the word "twn" ['of-the'] has been changed to the word "AND", which is really the Greek word "KAI" and not "TWN", and then let us put it all this (above information) together. First let us start with a verse in Revelation.

REVELATION 20:10

hEmeras	*kai nuktos eis tous*	*aiOnas*	*tOn*	*aiOnOn* (Grk)
ordealized	and night for the	eons	of-the	eons (LIT)
tormented	day and night for -- ever	*[and]*		ever. (KJV)
ordealized	day and night into the eons of the			eons. (CLV)

These are obviously false translations and rather more looked upon by etymologists as 'interpretations' than translations. They are not derived from an exact transliteration [a literal translation], but are interpretive glosses put over the real meanings. It appears that they are purposed frauds! No simple minded Greek scholar would dare make such mistakes. But, intelligent Nicolaitan Baal-Lords, and pagan Sun priests would,.

Well, first of all, Hell and the Lake of Fire are not the same and have nothing in common except that they BOTH only exist "for-the EONS of-the EONS". Without this understanding of limited time designations, though un-designated, yet surely limited, we get a false concept that they both never end. Even though both had a beginning, and in some passages it is shown they all have an end, the theologians still pawn off the idea that the flames burn forever and the damned suffer eternally. "Bah, Humbug!"

If there is a true definition of the false Gospel hatched by the Devil, as Paul warned about, it cannot possibly be an evangel that teaches the universal reconciliation of all mankind "in Christ" where Christ is heir to everything, and the Devil gets nothing. The false gospel mentioned by The Apostle Paul cannot possibly be a gospel teaching the universal reconciliation of all mankind. It cannot possibly be a gospel of unlimited atonement. It can only be a lying false gospel of "limited atonement." For, what benefit would Satan gain from such a teaching, and how would this facilitate his placing his throne above God's, if all end up in God's hands? You cannot have a throne with a King upon it, and it be a real throne and a real King with any supremacy, when there are no subjects. The throne which commands the most subjects is the throne that sits above all other thrones. Now, what do we have with contemporary traditional limited atonement theories? It is no stretch of the imagination, that the devil teaches a gospel that ends with Christ. This is the basic framework of the plan of the ages of God.

Ps. 49:15   SOULS RANSOMED FROM HELL

"Surely Elohim, He shall ransom my soul from the hand of the unseen ('shaul' = Hell) that (for) He shall take me." (CLV)

["But God WILL redeem my soul ["psyche" = mind, consciousness, being] from the power of the grave [Hell = "a hole"; Hades; "the unseen realm"]: for He shall [WILL] receive me. Selah."]

As odd as this may sound, God purposes even to redeem the damned from Hell. This is such a refutation to the traditional teaching that all souls entering HELL ("Hades," "the Grave") are entering with a one-way (free) ticket. In this verse, the Psalmist, like the Universalist today, is telling its readers to trust God that He will redeem souls even from the power of the grave and receive these souls (beings) back into His hands. This must have been based upon a "grave" question in those days just as it is today. This is more evidence against a never ending Hell.

This is such a refutation to the traditional teaching that all souls entering HELL ("Hades," "the Grave") are entering with a one-way prepaid ticket. Rather, the Psalmist is telling us to trust God that He will redeem our souls from the power of the grave and receive us back into His hands. This is more evidence against a never ending Hell. The following verse further supports this.

Hosea 13:14   PURPOSE TO REDEEMED ALL FROM SHEOL - (HELL)

"I will ransom them from the power of the grave (Hell); I will redeem them from death: O death, I will be thy plagues; O grave (Hell), I will be thy destruction: repentance shall be hid from mine eyes." (KJV)

["I WILL ransom them from the power of the grave [Hell = Sheol = Hades, 'unseen realm']; I WILL redeem them from death: O' Death, I WILL be thy [death's] plagues; O' Grave [SHEOL, Hell], I WILL be thy [death & the grave's] destruction."]

The Hebrew literal translation has God the destroyer of death and Hell, AFTER He redeems all men from them. The Book of Revelation supports this verse by saying: "And the sea gave up the dead who were in it; and death and Hell delivered up the dead who were in them: and they were judged every man according to their works" (Rev. 20:13).

Notice also that this judgment day is a judgment of the "works of men," not of a man's salvation! The word Sheol was often translated "Hell" in the Authorized Version In later English translations, it was wisely changed to some another word like "death," "the grave," or simply the transliterated Hebrew word Sheol. It refers to the unseen status of the dead and has nothing to do with the English concept of "hell." Since many of the dead have died of diseases and all of them have experienced "destruction" from the land of the living, **Hosea 13:14** seems to be God's battle cry heralding the demise of death.

In II Timothy 1:10 it is said that Christ "abolished" death. Hebrews 2:15 tells us that the power of death and the devil himself were destroyed through Christ. The Apostle Paul quoted **Hosea 13:14** in I Corinthians 15:54 and said that death has a "sting," that its sting is SIN, and the victory over death was accomplished through Christ. -- [HOWE]

Is. 51:11 ALL RANSOMED RETURN

"The ones being ransomed of Yahweh, they shall return and they shall enter Zion in jubilation; and rejoicing for the Age is on their head. Elation and rejoicing shall overtake them, and affliction shall flee, and grief and sighing."

The redeemed (the ones being ransomed = all men) of the (that belong to) LORD shall (WILL) return, and come with singing unto Zion; and everlasting (age-lasting) joy (shall be) (WILL be) upon their head(s): they shall (WILL) obtain gladness and joy; (and) sorrow and mourning shall (WILL) flee away.

The verse is very clear as to what will happen. Some suppose this only applies to some select (few) people, the Jews?, some portion of the gentiles?, or maybe only the especially believing good churchmen? If all pronouns are considered to be equivalent to "all mankind" then it is easily seen that the jubilation in Zion here mentioned is in reference to the entire human race. After all, who is it that Yahweh is willing to be ransomed? Who are "the ones," the "they," the "their," and the "them's?" If you are reading this, it is referring to you! Now, go tell all others of this good news of the redemption of Christ.

The redeemed (the ones being ransomed = all men) of the (that belong to) LORD shall (WILL) return, and come with singing unto Zion; and everlasting (age-lasting) joy (shall be) (WILL be) upon their head(s): they shall (WILL) obtain gladness and joy; (and) sorrow and mourning shall (WILL) flee away.

THE JUDGEMENT OF GOD WHO RECONCILES ALL - JUDGMENT IS NOT "FOREVER"

Tradition teaches the wicked and disobedient will be exposed to the anger and wrath of God, "forever." .i.e. they will burn in the pit of fire for eternity, and forever separated from God. But, this not only degrades God's mercy in judgement, but contradicts God's omnipresence.   God's wrath is not something separate from God, but is God Himself correcting sin and evil.

2 Sam. 14.14   GOD'S WRATH IS NOT FOREVER

Perpetual chastisement is a false teaching. It does not matter how you slice the cake, if a father were to beat his child perpetually, he would be locked up! What human would say that it is just to punish your child forever? There are rare exceptions locked up behind bars.

"And He [God] devised means so as not to keep expelled the one who is expelled by Him."

"For we must needs die, and [are] as water spilt on the ground, which cannot be gathered up again; neither doth God respect [any] person: yet doth He devise means, that his banished be not expelled from him." (AV)

"for we do surely die, and [are] as water which is running down to the earth, which is not gathered, and Elohim does not accept a person, and has devised devices in that the outcast is not outcast by Him." (CLV)

God is not interested in perpetual chastisement. Joab had called for a "wise woman" from Tekoa to enact a skit before King David in which she would pretend to be seeking David's protection for her son who, she would say, had killed his brother in a fight. She told David that the remaining son's life was being threatened for his action. Believing that the story was true, David promised safety for her living boy. The act was a very clever drama, parallel to a recent event in which David had banished his own son Absolom for killing his brother Amnon. The woman applied the story to David by asking him why He was banishing Absolom. In her final brief lecture to the king, she stated that even God creates devices by which people being disciplined by Him are not completely expelled. No criticism of her statement about God was made in this passage or elsewhere in the Bible. The account suggests that God is not interested in perpetual chastisement and that He would surely not use everlasting separation in hell as a punishment for lost souls. -- [G. HOWE]

Jer. 3: 5   HIS ANGER IS NOT FOREVER

"WILL He reserve His anger forever [for the ages, and beyond]? [On the other hand,] WILL He [possibly] keep it to the end [of the ages]?"

Will He maintain it forever? This is a rhetorical question. Of course, God will not maintain His anger and judgment forever, for He would be as much a slave to that anger as those whom He supposedly damns. This is answered and proved in the following verses.

Jer. 3:12

"I am merciful, saith the Lord, and I WILL not keep my anger forever."

In addition, what anger is this but the supposed anger of "eternal damnation" taught over the last fifteen hundred years?

Lam. 3: 31-33   GOD DOES NOT CAST OFF FOREVER

"For the Lord WILL not cast off [mankind] forever; but though He causes grief, yet WILL He have compassion [on ALL the human race] according to the multitude of His mercies: for He doth not afflict willingly, nor grieve the children of mankind [forever]."

Obviously, it is not the children's fault, but Adam's.

"From this we learn that God often punishes, or afflicts, to humble the proud spirit, and when we allow his visitations to lead us to repentance, He restores us according to the multitude of his mercies, by which He treats us better than we deserve, and "will not cast off forever." -- [AUSTIN]

Ps. 30:5   GOD'S ANGER IS ONLY FOR A MOMENT

"For his anger [endureth but] a [twinkling] moment; in his favor [is] life: weeping may endure for a night, but joy [cometh] in the morning." (AV)

This verse presents a typology between two concepts: God's

anger, wrath, or damnation on man and His mercy, forgiveness or gift of joy. Each is "timed" by the imagery used. His anger is "but for a moment," while His Joy lasts a whole day or longer - the texts does not put an end on the Joy, but suggests it is as like a lifetime and longer. This verse teaches that damnation (weeping) is short compared to Joy, which is actually never ending. The second set of images further illustrates this point. All the negative images are for a short moment - a twinkling - as compared to Joy lasting for life. The meaning is that God's anger against men lasts only as long as the eons, whereas, "in the morning" [AFTER the resurrection and eons are over], His Glad Tidings of Great Joy towards all men continues and never ceases. This "in the morning" appears to be a descriptive expression of "THAT DAY" when Christ brings us ALL that new painless, happy, resurrected FINAL STATE. If chastening for SIN lasted forever, Psalm 30:5 would be in error. A brief history of God's dealings with humankind goes something like this: indignation, lamentation, confession, and then jubilation. A joyful finale awaits everybody "in the morning. -- [G. HOWE]

Gods judgment and the damnation of men is but for a short age-lasting duration. However, the new joyous resurrection life He has promised us all after the eons are over will never end.

Ps. 77:7-9 GOD'S LOVE DOES NOT END

"Will my Lord cast off for the ages? In addition, will He be accepting no more? Has His unfailing love ended permanently? Has His promise from generation to generation failed? Has God forgotten to be merciful? Or was He in anger shut off His compassion?"

Asaph posed six rhetorical questions, each of which deserves "No" as a resounding answer. They demonstrate that even during indignation, God never fails to exude unfailing love, faithfulness, benevolence, graciousness, and favor. God's dealings with lost dead people will surely have salutary and remedial effects, as verified in Lamentations 3:31-33 and Isaiah 57:16. -- [G. HOWE]

Is. 54:8 GOD'S MERCY EQUALLY APPLIED TO ALL

"In a little wrath I hid my face from thee for a moment; but with age-enduring kindness WILL I have mercy on all mankind, saith the Lord, all humanity's Redeemer." (CLV)

Is. 57:15-16   GOD'S WRATH NOT FOREVER

"I WILL not contend forever [for all the ages], neither WILL I be always wroth: [why?] For the spirit should [then] fail before me, and the human souls which I have made [WOULD be lost forever]."

Many theologians attempt to explain away the force of this great truth asserted by the Prophet. They insist that the preceding verse limits this declaration to a certain class, viz: "the contrite and humble." "I dwell in the high and holy place, with him also that is of a contrite and humble spirit, to revive the spirit of the humble, and to revive the heart of the contrite ones " (v. 15)

They say that the verse is not "unconditionally" applicable to all men. For, this supposition would contradict the scope of the context, and its plainly expressed language. The 15th verse fixes, they insist, the application of the quotation to the "humble spirit"—to "the contrite ones.'" Our Lord in Matt. 5:4 explains this: He said, "Blessed are they that mourn, for they shall be comforted." That the passage does not apply indiscriminately to all men. It is evident from verses 20 and 21, that the wicked are destitute of peace, in opposition to the "contrite ones," with whom the Lord will not contend forever.

Yet, it is difficult to see in what sense this verse can limit the application of the assurance that God will not contend forever. Rather, it is very certainly clear the Most High did not mean to say simply that He would not contend forever with the "contrite and humble." When we give the passage the plain construction required by the laws of language, and the dictates of good sense, its meaning becomes abundantly evident.   Contrary to eternal tormentors, The Creator, after stating that He dwells with the contrite and humble, goes on to reveal an infinitely important fact in relation to all men, viz: that He is not an enemy to any of the creatures He has formed. Although He will punish them justly for their sins, He will not war with them nor tear them in pieces, as a bloodthirsty savage, or as the fierce hyena destroy their victims. This was the momentous truth He aimed to impress upon the hearts of men. He designed to instruct them that He acted on higher and better principles than the sanguinary gods of the surrounding heathen nations.

The priests of these gods taught that they would bless their followers only, while they would pour out wrath and torment upon their enemies forever! However, the true God holds the tender relationship of Father to all his creatures, and his proceedings with them are characterized by principles entirely different from those, which govern Pagan idols. That this is the entire meaning and spirit of the passage is evident not only from the structure of the language itself, but also from the succeeding verses. "At his depravity, for a moment, I was wroth, and I am smiting him. And I conceal My face from him and am wroth when He is going, backsliding in the way of his heart. His ways I see, and I will heal him and comfort him, and I will repay comfort to him and to his mourners." (v. 17, 18)

Here God plainly asserts that the principle of his government, is not like that of heathen deities, who punish simply to destroy; but He punishes to heal and restore the disobedient! How perfectly opponents of universal restoration pervert the language, which inculcates these high and beautiful principles, by their reconstruction of the passage. To have it teach such a doctrine, they must fasten upon it, allusions antithetical to what the prophet meant. "I will not contend forever, neither will I be always wroth, with the humble and contrite." Such as, "I WILL contend FOREVER, and I Will be ALWAYS wroth with the millions of my children, who fail to see and feel the light of truth in the brief span of this life!" Is there a man, endowed with ordinary perception, who can believe God designed to convey such an idea? -- [AUSTIN, Edited]

God revealed His intention not to punish endlessly and not to remain permanently indignant. In the face of Isaiah 57:16, how can so many believers cling to the concept of permanent torment and separation for lost souls? The reason God gave for not punishing endlessly is that the very spirits and souls of those under chastisement would grow faint. God's unfailing love will have the upper hand even in His contentions with sinful people being disciplined. -- [G. HOWE]

Jer. 30:23-24   THE NON-ETERNAL NATURE OF GOD'S WRATH

"Behold, the storm of the Lord will come forth in wrath,—a driving wind, swirling down on the heads of the wicked. The fierce anger of the Lord will not turn back UNTIL He has performed and fully accomplished the purposes of His heart. In the latter days you will understand this."

THE LITERAL Hebrew is much clearer in this: "Behold, a temptest of Yahweh, a fury she goes forth, a temptest swirling on the head(s) of the wicked-ones, He shall perforate (put it on their heads). He shall not turn back the heat of His anger UNTIL His doing and establishing - His carrying-out of His plans of His heart. In the hereafter (last) days you SHALL understand (consider or reconsider) (in-her, it) this! - [the limited judgment and universal restitution of all]."

Some Old Testament passages proclaiming God's ultimate salvation of all people are usually not quite as clear as the more than 20 free standing New Testament sections supporting the reconciliation of all. Nonetheless, the Old Testament verses give us a fore-view of what Christ, Paul, John, Peter, and James were going to proclaim. In speaking of God's wrath, for example, Jeremiah pointed toward reconciliation. This point is clear in almost any translation. God's wrath lasts only until He has performed his will [the purpose of His heart]. There is a hint here that the knowledge of how God would carry out only a "limited punishment" would be fully understood only in the "latter days." After hundreds of years of false teaching about everlasting torment, the concept of ultimate reconciliation for all people is finally gaining an audience in these "latter days" and this scripture is beingFULFILLEDbefore our eyes! -- [G. HOWE]

Jer. 23:20 and 30:24   END TIME PROPHECY OF SAVING ALL

"The anger of Yahweh will not turn back until He does and carries out the plan of His heart. In the latter days you will understand it fully."

Jeremiah 30:24 has exactly the same wording as Jeremiah 23:20, except that 30:24 has the word "fierce" or "burning" inserted before the word "anger." God's anger will continue until it establishes the goals that are on His heart. God's anger is purposeful and is no mere fit of rage. The objective of His indignation is to cause changes that are central to Him and His anger only continues until those missions have been accomplished. The fact that God's anger is burning (30:24) fits with the fact that God's Word is like a fire (See Jeremiah 23:29). I John chapter 4 states three times that "God is love." "In the latter days you will understand it fully," Jeremiah was told. Could this refer to Christ's coming and Paul's full revelation of reconciliation, both of which were far beyond the days of Jeremiah? -- [G. HOWE]

Heb. 12:5-11   DAMNATION IS LIMITED

Paul taught the limitation, remedial design, efficacious nature, and benevolent object of all the divine chastisements. "My son, despise not thou the chastening of the Lord, nor faint when thou art rebuked of him: for whom the Lord loveth He chasteneth, and scourgeth every son whom He receiveth. If ye endure chastening, God dealeth with you as with sons, for what son is He whom the father chasteneth not? But if ye be without chastisement, whereof all are partakers, then are ye bastards, and not sons. Furthermore, we have had fathers of our flesh who corrected us, and we gave them reverence: shall we not much rather be in subjection to the Father of spirits, and live? For they verily for a few days chastened us after their own pleasure; but He for our profit, that we might be partakers of his holiness. Now, no chastening for the present seemeth to be joyous, but grievous: nevertheless afterwards it yieldeth the peaceable fruits of righteousness unto them that are exercised thereby."

Hosea 14:4   GOD'S ANGER TURNS BACK

"I will heal their backsliding. I will love them freely. For My anger turns back from him."

The judgment of God results in healing, not in permanent punishment. We are assured that God's anger has a turning point beyond which all that remains is the love, which expressed itself earlier in the form of a cleansing anger.

Is.12:1-3   GOD'S ANGER REVERSED TO COMFORT

"You will say, in that day, 'I extol You, O Lord. You were angry with me and shall reverse Your anger and you shall comfort me. Behold, the Lord is my salvation, I will trust and will not be afraid. Yahweh is my strength and my song and He is becoming my salvation.' And with joy you draw water from the wells of salvation."

Probably all of Isaiah chapter 12 should be memorized because it is a proclamation of overwhelming joy for Israel, a joy that will flow across all the earth. Anger turns into comfort, strength, and singing. All people draw and drink the water of salvation joyfully. -- [G. HOWE]

Job 37:23   GOD DOES NOT OPPRESS FOREVER

"...in His [the Almighty's] justice and great righteousness, He does not oppress."

Elihu's Hebrew words have been rendered "He does not oppress" in the NIV and "He will not oppress" in the World English Bible. They have been given a similar translation in the NASB: "He will not afflict." Barnes commented as follows: "It is true that He did afflict people, but the idea is that there was not harshness or oppression in it." Any future use of cruel and everlasting punishments on lost people is precluded. Elihu's remark is but one of many phrases contradicting Augustine's theory of never-ending torment (see also Isaiah 57:16 and Lamentations 3:31-33). When evangelical believers fully understand that God does not oppress those who die outside of Christ, the clause "therefore men revere Him" in Job 37:23 will be more gloriously fulfilled. People will show even greater reverence to the One who has provided ultimate reconciliation for all humankind." -- [G. HOWE]

Joel 2:13 and 14a   GOD SLOW TO ANGER AND FULL OF LOVE

"And tear your heart and not your garments. And turn back to Yahweh your God. For gracious and compassionate is He, slow to anger and of abundant kindness. And He relents from sending disaster. Who knows, if He will turn back and regret and leave a blessing behind, a present and a drink offering of Yahweh your God?"

Many passages in the Old Testament repeatedly emphasize that God does not enjoy bringing judgment on people. He does not rejoice in His own adverse discipline and the correction He must bring is shown to be temporary, with God often "turning back" and sending blessings as a result. All of these passages militate against accepting the concept that He will be pleased to consign people who die outside of Christ to unending chastisement. -- [G. HOWE]

Lev. 26:43-44   GOD IS NOT ETERNALLY HATEFUL

"...they will pay for their sins . . . and yet, I reject them not and [I] loath them not, so as to finish them off and make void my covenant with them."

In Leviticus 26:43-44 the Bible deals with Israel and her upcoming captivity. Yet it is a bellwether lesson on how God will handle other people later on. His dealings with Israel and with New Testament believers are merely a "first fruits" (James 1:18) of His treatment for all humankind, a prelude to the greater final "harvest." Paying for SIN does not involve the sinner being abhorred. Putting a lost soul into everlasting torment, however, would violate God's words against hateful behavior, which He has flatly rejected. God avoided "...finishing them off..." because it would break a pledge that He had made specifically to Israel and more generally, to the human race. God never breaks any promise. - [G. HOWE]

PARABLE OF THE PRIEST AND THE CONGREGATION: THE GUILT OF ONE MAN IS NOT CAST UPON HIS CHILDREN OR OTHER PEOPLE

Numb.16:22

"... and [they] said [or asked] 'O God, the God of the spirits of all flesh, shall one man SIN, and [consequently] wilt thou be wroth [forever?] with all the congregation?"

Adam brought death upon all humankind. Now, what does the Bible say that Jesus did? Jesus brought "the free gift of life upon ALL men unto the justification of life" (Romans 5:18). He "takes away the SIN of the world" (John 1: 29). "It pleased the Father, that in Jesus, should ALL fullness dwell" (Col.1:19), which is to say that the promise to Abraham is to be FULFILLED with "all things"...given to Christ (Jn. 16:15). We see, In Romans 5:19 that as "the many became sinners," even so, Christ came to take away that SIN of "the many" - the SIN of the world.

This is the answer to the question put to God in the Book of Numbers, which tells us that God is not wroth forever with all mankind, because of one [another] man's SIN. Modern theologians deny this and twist the Scriptures to teach the contrary, that all humans are born to suffer the guilt of the first father, Adam.

The above verse shows us that God casts not the SIN(s) of the father(s) upon the children. This analogy types Adam as the priest, who sinned and the rest of the human race is called "the congregation." It appears that the ultimate responsibility of "all" is on the "head of the congregation" in the eyes of God (Adam and Christ) and not with the congregation [i. e. "all mankind"].

Apparently, the question of the final destiny of all mankind is not a new one. The question is rhetorical and has built into it the answer: "Of course not, my wrath will not abide forever" (**Ps. 103: 9**). For, no one stays in Hell forever (Rev. 20:13, **Ps. 49:15**, and Job 14:13). But, many of those unsaved will suffer "age-lasting" correction, while the ones made righteous by God "in Christ" will immediately abide with Him during the intermediate state (Philip. 1:23).

Salvation from Hell (Hades, the Grave, and Sheol) surly is a responsibility of man to avoid, but this is quite different from the universal reconciliation of the All, which is the sole responsibility of Christ. Christ overturns the Adamic curse upon humankind. Adam brought death upon the entire human race within the eons.

Now, what does the Bible say that Jesus did to reverse the wrath of His father from mankind? Jesus brought "the free gift of life to ALL men unto the justification of life" (Romans 5:18). He "takes away the sin [SINGULAR!] of the world" (Jn. 1: 29).

"It pleased the Father, that in Jesus, should ALL fullness dwell" (Col. 1·19), which is to say that the promise given to Abraham is to be FULFILLED with "all things"given to Christ (Jn. 16:15). We see, In Romans 5:19 that as "the many became sinners," even so, Christ came to take away that SIN of "the many" - the SIN of the world.

This is the answer to the question put to God in the Book of Numbers, which tells us that God is not wroth forever with "all mankind." because of one man's SIN, as modern theologians promote.

The majority of churches press a false evangel that each human is responsible for his ultimate and final "eternal" destiny; for they say, the Bible teaches "individual accountability" or "responsibility." Human responsibility is true as to immediate destiny, but when it comes to ultimate destiny, this is the sole responsibility of God. Man is responsible whether He goes to be immediately with Christ or not, for God "makes" no one go there. He does not "force" one to believe. The ability given to man, when He "hears the Preacher" and after He "hears the Evangel" to confess with the mouth (Rom. 10:9) and believe in his heart, that Jesus died and rose from the dead places in him this responsibility. He may either quickly see and believe or resist to some degree, even to the point of passing from this life without believing.

Yet, mankind has no say as to ultimate universal reconciliation. In this case, it is God that is solely responsible and thus draws "ALL men unto Himself" (Jn.12:32). Hence, the consequence is that every tongue will confess and every knee will bend (Rom. 14:11, Is. 45:23). It is God who "worketh all in all" (1 Cor. 12:6) and who works the All after His will (Eph.1:11), so He may be the ALL in all (1 Cor. 15:28).

God has determined this great reconciliation of ALL His creation and man will surly and freely bend, and bow, and be thankful for this. No "congregation member" has upon them perpetually abiding wrath, for God is the owner of the spirits of all flesh, and does not hold His wrath on them indefinitely. He plainly shows us in this verse that it is short term, and only for the Eons, and not beyond.

Jn. 3:18   JUDGED, BUT NOT ETERNALLY DAMNED

ho   pisteuOn   eis auton ou   krinetai
THE one-BELIEVING INTO Him NOT IS-beING-JUDGED
ho   de   mE   pisteuOn   EdE
kekritai THE YET NO one-BELIEVING ALREADY has-been JUDGED
hoti   mE pepisteuken   eis   to   onoma tou
that   NO He-HAS-BELIEVED INTO THE NAME OF-THE
monogenous   huiou   tou   theou
ONLY-generated   SON   OF-THE   God.

LITERAL TRANSLATION:

"The [Person]-Believing into Him, is being Judged NOT;
yet, the [Person]-Believing NOT [into Him], HAS-been-JUDGED
ALREADY, [In]-that, He-HAS-BELIEVED NO(t), into the Name
of-the ONLY-generated Son of God."

This is a favorite verse used by some of the limited atonement 'snake-oil' preachers to push the idea that there is an eternal difference between those "not being judged" and those "already being judged ." In other words, according to Authorized Version supporters, one group is damned forever, while the other ELECTED are blessed forever. But, as we analyze this verse, there is NO ,mention or indication as to any final destiny. What will be observed, if one ceases and desist drinking the snake water, only a difference between persons, and the condition of being judged. In the Greek, the word "condemned" is "krinetai," which means "IS-beING-JUDGED." Our use of the word condemned is soaked with the stigma of "DAMNED," which to us seems to mean, "Destined to burn in Hell for Eternity". This is absolutely wrong! Being "judged" can in no way mean sentenced to Hell, for notice that EVERYONE at one time (before conversion) was someone who was "BELIEVING NOT ." Therefore, they would be one of those that "HAS-been-JUDGED ALREADY ." If being "JUDGED ALREADY" means DAMNED with no way to obtain redemption, then we have a contradiction. If this snake-oil teaching were true, NO ONE could become saved, for they would be "ALREADY JUDGED" (i.e. DAMNED') -- signed, sealed and delivered to Hell, way before their physical deaths, and could not possibly become one of those who is believing INTO His Name. Thus, this verse does NOT teach the Divine pre-ordination of many to eternal damnation, who are not elect. What it does infer is, that there are many not yet "within" the election process.

Many use this verse to teach a "LIMITED ATONEMENT," that Jesus Christ's death on the Cross had nothing whatsoever to do for the sins OF THE WORLD. These people believe, on the contrary, that Christ's death was exclusively for the "elect" or those who find themselves to be Christians. The REASON that God would condemn the non-elect to hell in this case would be BECAUSE CHRIST HAD NOT DIED FOR THEIR sins. But, the Bible says, that Christ DID died for the SIN of the World.

The ONLY SIN that has one in a state of being "JUDGED ALREADY," is the SIN of "NOT BELIEVING" in the Lord Jesus Christ. The verse says, "He that BELIEVETH NOT is JUDGED ALREADY ," and this is only because He has yet to believe in Christ, the Son of God. The person mentioned in this verse is not "JUDGED ALREADY" because Christ did not die for his sins, but He IS JUDGED ALREAY because He "has believe not" in the Christ, who DID die for every one of his sins on the cross! It becomes, therefore, not a question of SIN, but a question as to the awareness of people as to who Jesus is and what He did -- the sins of the world having already been atoned for and paid for by Jesus Christ's death at the cross. All that remains is for the sinner, is the TRUST and FAITH that is needed in this Savior! And, this is WILLED to be so by God and shall be testified in due time, in the EONS to come.

GLAD TIDINGS PROMISES
TO DESTROY THE DEVILS WORKS

Heb. 2:14, 15, and 1 Jn. 3:8   PROMISE TO DESTROY THE DEVILS WORKS

"Forasmuch, then, as the children are partakers of flesh and blood, He, also, himself (i.e., Christ), took part of the same, that through death He might destroy him that had the power of death — that is, the devil and deliver all mankind who through fear of death were all their life-time subject to bondage."

Jesus will not only destroy the devil, but He will destroy all his works. "For this purpose the Son of God was manifested, that He might destroy the works of the devil." I John 3:8. The reign of all evil, then, is to cease; the Prince of Peace is to be its conqueror. How false, then, is the notion that SIN and misery will continue forever! -- [MANFORD]

1 Jn. 3.8   MEN ARE NOT THE DEVILS WORKS

"He that committeth SIN is of the devil, for the devil sinneth from the beginning. For this purpose the Son of God was manifested, that He might destroy the works of the devil."

Christ destroys the works of the Devil, not men! Let us analyze this verse. Whoever sins is of the devil. All men SIN. Thus, all men are of the devil. For, men SIN because the devil sinned from the beginning. He persuaded man to SIN. Since then, all men SIN after the devil. This was the "work" of the devil. Men cannot help but SIN. Now, it was for this, that Christ was purposed, that He come to destroy this work of the devil, not destroy the man, but the "work" or "effects" of the devil. There is no mention here that Jesus came to destroy men. He actually said, that He came not to condemn that which was lost because of the work of the devil, but to SAVE that which was lost because of this work of the devil. Such simple logic. -- [MANFORD]

CHRIST DESTROYS ALL SIN OF THE WORLD

Hosea 10:8   ALL ISRAEL'S SIN DESTROYED

"The high places also of Aven, the SIN of Israel, shall be destroyed: the thorn and the thistle shall come up on their altars;

and they shall say to the mountains, Cover us; and to the hills, fall on us." (KJV)

Jn. 1:29

"Behold the Lamb of God, which taketh away the SIN of the [whole] world." [I.e. all mankind]

Heb. 9:26

"since then He ǀ must often be suffering from the disruption of the world, yet now, once, (when) at the conclusion of these   eons, for the repudiation of (the world's) SIN through His sacrifice, is He ǀwas He; He was purposed to be] manifest." (CLV)

"For then must He often have suffered since the foundation of the world: but now once in the end of the world hath He appeared to put away SIN by the sacrifice of himself." (AV)

In Rom. 11:32 God hardens the hearts of   ALL humans so as to loosen their hearts later, so as to save all of them. We can at least admit that, God is explaining to us that He locks ALL humans in a type of stubbornness, so that He can later be universally merciful to them all. It appears that All this human opposition to God's will, He changes later, when SIN is set aside and when the Son of God has untied all of the devil's works, as He intends to do. God reverses what He said He has done in Rom 11:32. See (I John 3:8). We cannot really fully understand why He does this, but we CAN understand THAT He does it and equally so with ALL. Here, the word "sin" is in the singular tense and refers to ALL the SIN of the whole world. Now, does not SIN only reside IN humans? It is a heresy to say SIN is in material objects or matter substance. Thus, Christ repudiates all the SIN of the human world. Therefore, we have here a direct statement of universal reconciliation of all mankind.

PROMISES DEATH & HELL DESTROYED

Rev. 20:13   DEATH AND HELL NOT ETERNAL

"And the sea gave up the dead which were in it; and death and hell delivered up the dead which were in them: and they were judged every man according to their works."

Rev. 20:14   DEATH AND HELL PUT TO NO USE

"And death and hell [without the occupants] were cast into the lake of fire. This is the second death:" [i. e. the death or END OF hell and death: the utter destruction of death and all that bears that name.]

2 Tim. 1:10   NO SUCH THING AS ETERNAL DEATH

"Christ hath abolished death, and hath brought life and immortality to light through the Gospel."

Observe here that Christ did not bring eternal death and an endless hell to light. He revealed life and immortality for our race beyond the grave. This is a very important declaration, and in no part of the Bible is it contradicted. Remember, temporal death is the last enemy man will ever encounter, and that is to be destroyed by the Lord Omnipotent. Amen. -- [MANFORD]

1 Cor. 15:55   DEATH HAS NO MORE STING

"O death, where is thy sling? O grave, [hades, hell,] where is thy victory?"

1 Cor. 15:56

"The sting of death is SIN; and the strength of SIN is the law."

I Cor. 15:57

"But thanks be to God, who giveth MANKIND the victory through OUR Lord Jesus Christ."

1 Cor. 15. 26;   and   2 Tim. 1.10;   Heb. 2.4, 15

This is an additional evidence that Paul speaks of a universal resurrection, for as Dr. Clarke says, in commenting on this passage: "But death cannot be destroyed by there being no further death; death can only be destroyed and annihilated by a general resurrection; and if there be no general resurrection it is not evident that death will retain his empire. Therefore, the fact that death shall be destroyed, assures the fact that there shall be a general resurrection; and this is a proof, also, that after the resurrection, there shall be no more death."

The Doctor is undoubtedly correct – there will be NO MORE DEATH AFTER THE GENERAL RESURRECTION, for death will be swallowed up in eternal Life [EONIAN = 'Lasting Into the Eons and Beyond']. Why then, do men threaten their fellow men with "eternal death," with a "death that never dies," beyond the resurrection? Paul knew nothing of such a death. Remark also, that temporal death is man's last enemy. Before we encounter death we have many enemies to grapple with. SIN, temptation, and suffering beset us from the cradle to the grave; but death is the last of the series and Almighty God will destroy that one. But this is not the common opinion. It is supposed by some that when death shall be destroyed, a large part of mankind will have innumerable enemies to encounter – that God, Christ and all the angels of heaven, and all the devils in hell will be their enemies. But this is a mistake, for death is the last enemy, and there can surely be no enemy beyond the last. -- [MANFORD]

Paul teaches the subjection all the enemies of God and man and the final destruction of the last enemy, death. 1 Cor. 15:26, "The last enemy shall be destroyed, death." 2 Tim. 1:10, "Who hath abolished death, and brought life and immortality to light." Death is here declared to be the last of all the enemies. If death is the last enemy, certainly there can be no enemy after death. And if the last enemy, death, is eventually destroyed, then man will have no more enemies. When this time arrives, when man will have no enemy, what will prevent his being ultimately holy and happy?

Paul not only teaches the destruction of death, but He also teaches the destruction of that which has the power of death, and the final deliverance of those who through fear of death were all their lifetime subject to bondage. (Heb. 2:4, 15), "Forasmuch then as the children are partakers of flesh and blood, He also himself likewise took part of the same; that through death He might destroy him that had the power of death, that is, the devil; and deliver them who through fear of death were all their lifetime subject to bondage." What has the power of death? Answer: "sin, when it is finished, bringeth forth death." (James 1:15)

SIN, then, according to the apostle, is eventually to be destroyed and banished from the universe of God. "OUR" = 'all mankind'. He has died to slay death: He has risen again to bring all mankind out from under the Empire of Hades. "And death and hell delivered up the dead which were in them." (Rev. 20:13)

All this He has done through His mere unmerited mercy; and eternal thanks are due to God for this unspeakable gift. He has given MANKIND the victory over SIN, Satan, death, the grave, and hell. -- [Dr. Adam Clarke. Edited]

Ps. 103:4 REDEEMED FROM RUINATION

God, "Who is redeeming your life from ruin, Who is crowning you with benignity and compassion."

God is the Savior, Who is redeeming humanity's life from destruction, Who is crowning humanity with loving kindness and tender mercies. This is a universally applied crowning, for all men, and especially, but not exclusively, for those that believe.

Hosea 13:14 REDEEMED FROM SHEOL - (HELL)

"I will ransom them from the power of the grave; I will redeem them from death: O death, I will be thy plagues; O grave, I will be thy destruction: repentance shall be hid from mine eyes."(KJV)

"I WILL ransom them from the power of the grave [Hell = Sheol = Hades, 'unseen realm']; I WILL redeem them from death: O' Death, I WILL be thy [death's] plagues; O' Grave [SHEOL, Hell], I WILL be thy [death & the grave's] destruction."

The Hebrew literal translation has God the destroyer of death and Hell, AFTER He redeems all men from them. The Book of Revelation supports this verse by saying: "And the sea gave up the dead who were in it; and death and hell delivered up the dead who were in them: and they were judged every man according to their works" (Rev. 20:13). [Notice also that this judgment day is a judgment of the "works of men," not a man's salvation!] The word Sheol was often translated "hell" in the Authorized Version In later English translations, it was wisely changed to some another word like "death," "the grave," or simply the transliterated Hebrew word Sheol. It refers to the unseen status of the dead and has nothing to do with the English concept of "hell." Since many of the dead have died of diseases and all of them have experienced "destruction" from the land of the living, Hosea 13:14 is God's battle cry heralding the demise of death. In II Timothy 1:10 it is said that Christ "abolished" death. Hebrews 2:15 tells us that the power of death and the devil himself were destroyed through Chrithe Apostle Paul quoted Hosea 13:14 in I Corinthians 15:54 and said that death has a "sting," that its sting is SIN, and the victory over death was accomplished through Christ. -- [HOWE]

Let the light of inspiration guide us. The Apostle Paul applies these words to the resurrection of the dead, at the last day, **1 Cor. 15:54, 55.** At the resurrection of the dead, then, God will destroy Sheol, "Hell". He does not raise his creatures from the dead in Sheol in order to again punish them forever back in Sheol, for Sheol shall then be destroyed. And neither does He do this in the Lake of Divine PUR-ification - (Lake of Fire).

Rom. 11:15 BRINGS LIFE FROM AMONG THE DEAD

"For if the casting away of them (Israel) [be] *the reconciling the world* [of mankind], *what* [WILL] *the receiving* [of them back be], *but life* [for all humans] *from the dead'?"*

All of Israel was cast aside for the purpose of "conciliating the whole World." The receiving of them back (for they are part of the conciliation of the World too) will be LIFE raised out from among the dead. Here is the logic, as scripture details: 1.) All the world was lost through what Adam did. 2.) God chose Israel to use as a people and so for purposes of bringing in the Promise to Abraham, God blinded and cast away Israel. 3.) God send Christ to bring reconciliation to man. The whole World was conciliated in what Christ did. 4.) Israel was blinded so that the Gentile could see. 5.) The Grace Age brings in conciliation to both Jew and Gentile alike, so that eventually God give sight back to Israel. 6.) Israel comes to see the Light and their messiah, and so ALL Israel will be saved. 7.) And so, ALL the Nations, all the Gentiles, all people, all flesh, and all humankind shall eventually be saved.

1 Thess. 5:9 None appointed unto permanent wrath

"God hath not appointed us to wrath, but to obtain salvation through our Lord Jesus Christ."

This language is addressed specially and entirely to Christians. This is evident from the fifth, verse, when, after having described certain characters, who cry peace, when "sudden destruction cometh upon them," he says, "ye are all the children of light, and the children of the day: we are not of the night nor of darkness."

It is also true in a general sense, for Paul uses the phrase "to obtain salvation." In a general sense, most have not obtained salvation, yet will obtain it, because they are appointed not to wrath, but to salvation. Thus, the word "us" in this passage refers to humanity in general, though the verse is directed to the believer. We might understand the verse better if we paraphrase it: "God hath not appointed [any of] us [humans] to [perpetual] wrath, but [rather, according to His promise to Abraham] to obtain salvation through our [us believers] Lord Jesus Christ." God has not appointed any man to wrath, but to obtain salvation, on condition that they embrace the gospel by a holy, soul-purifying faith." And we know that all will obtain this, for every man has been given a measure of faith. It is just a matter of timing in God's will as to when they will believe.

Individual human responsibility to believe is a Biblical truth, but let us analysis this verse in light of the entire Canon's context and extract further clarification as to what is being really being said. First, we must agree that this is addressed to Christians at the time, but we must also understand that it is not speaking about them only. If it was speaking about believers only and none other, then there would be no reason for Paul to add that they needed "to obtain salvation," (future tense) for they already had been saved. We must ask who Paul is speaking of when he uses the word "us". This word must include both believers and none believers or those "yet still sinners". Just as those believers who were believing, at one time were, in times past, "still yet sinners" and then got saved. Even so, it must extend to those still yet to believe.

If we split the verse into two statements we will see that we have a generally applied (anticipated) salvation of all, based upon a universally applied atonement that is known specifically by believers, where the atonement is understood with the knowledge that it is through "our" Lord Jesus Christ. One cannot help but understand this to mean: "God has not appointed us [all mankind] to wrath." But, "God has [rather] appointed us [all mankind] to obtain salvation through our Lord, [who we believers know is] Jesus Christ." This now fits very comfortably within the context of Christ's "drawing ALL towards himself" in His resurrection. Otherwise, His drawing all is not a drawing all, and thus is an empty promise. This statement that Paul addressed to Christians is to be understood to include all those other people ["neighbors", whom we are supposed to love as brothers], who are yet to "embrace the gospel by a holy, soul-purifying faith."

Surly, the word "us" here refers to all mankind, for Paul distinguishes this by showing that many still need to obtain salvation. Now, the statement is addressed 'to" believers, who should be understanding this, rather than questioning God's "common grace" for all humans as they still do today. We should suspect, that Paul is making a universal reconciliation statement to correct the false beliefs of his times, who were assuming that many others were not appointed to obtain salvation. It is not far removed from the false belief system of today.

Many people still believe that they are not only "special", but solely chosen at the exclusion of others. Paul corrects them by saying that no one is being appointed unto wrath permanently, like some false teachers were saying, but that all men are appointed to salvation. It is not such a far stretch to assume that Paul understood the same gospel message as St. Luke, when he told us that, "all flesh shall see the salvation of God" (Lk. 3:6).

Jn. 12:32   Christ DRAGS all men to Himself

hupsOthO   ek   tEs   gEs   pantas   helkusO
I be lifted up out   of-the   earth, ALL,   I-shall-be-drawing,

pros   emauton
toward   Myself

St. John continues to say, *"And this He said signifying by what kind of death He was about to die."* Christ proclaimed that if He died on the cross, He would be drawing all [meaning all people] to Himself. Some say this means, that in Christ's judgment all are drawn to Him and He will separate the believers from those who rejected Him, giving to each a permanent sentence. Others propose that these are words coming directly from the mouth of the Messiah and they confirm that based on His crucifixion, He intends to save everybody who ever lived. What do you think Christ meant in saying, "I shall be drawing all unto Myself"?

A central contention that has divided the Church for generations has been the misunderstood teachings of election and man's free-will. The battle between these two ideas revolves around who chooses and who is redeemed. Does God choose man or does man choose God? This has created two major camps – those who say God calls all to be saved, but only chooses (elects) a few -- and those who say God desires all to be saved, but is only "able" to save a few. Very few people now days consider the Biblical position, --   that God said He wills (calls ALL) and draws each man (chooses every man in due time, throughout the ages, according to His Divine good pleasure) to be saved, because He originally "purposed" all men to a perfect life of fellowship with Him.

Just how many are purposed to be raised up from the dead, restored to life and to come to bow before God? Contrary to popular opinion and church tradition, "every knee shall bow." Many other promise verses say He will surely accomplish this purpose. This is the Great Hope we should all be looking for. God calls all and saves all, electing a few, and eventually all along the way; for He desires all, is drawing all, and therefore will save all, because He has "planned" to save all.

Eccl. 12:7   ALL SPIRITS WILL RETURN TO GOD
"*And the dust returns to the earth, as it was, and the spirit returns to God, Who gave it.*"

When a lost person dies, their spirit is not forever separated from God. To the contrary, God, Who is the giver of all human spirits, gets them all back, no exceptions. The reason this is true is, because God is the God of all spirits. He is the Father and owner of all spirits. (**Heb. 12:9**) "...Elohim of the spirits for all flesh, as for the one man, He is sinning; but shall You be wrathful over the whole congregation?" (CLV) "... O God, the God of the spirits of all flesh, shall one man SIN, and wilt thou be wroth with all the congregation?" (AV) (also Nu. 16:22) -- [HOWE] The obvious answer to this question about what Adam is God is not wroth forever with the congregation (all descendants of Adam). The priest is as to Adam as the congregation is to all mankind.

Jn. 16:15
"*ALL that the Father hath are mine.*" - KJV

Seems that the Father has ALL 'everyone', and gives them to Christ.

Jn. 17:10
"*And ALL mine are thine, and thine are mine.*" - KJV

Ps. 22:29   ALL THE DEAD WILL THEN BOW
"*All [they that be] fat upon earth shall eat and worship: ALL they that go down to the dust shall bow before him.*" (AV)

The word "all" (pantas) in **John 12:32** is not clarified and obviously does not need to be, for ALL means all, not only of all creation, but also of all living beings. It would put limitations on the word all if it said, "*all the elect,*" "*only all those whosoever willeth,*" "*all God's favorites*" or "*all MEN that believe.*" But, the verse does not clarify any limitation. It clearly states all of humanity by saying that Christ shall be "***drawing all,***" which means EVERYTHING.

This would of course include all human beings that ever lived. The verse has no meaning otherwise. Apparently, this statement is analogous to the following: "*Then shall the dust return to the earth as it was; but the spirit shall return unto God who gave it*" (**Eccl. 12:7**). From these three passages we learn, that mankind is of divine origin; and, while on earth, under divine protection; and when leaving this world, eventually return to that great and good Being who created and sustains them.

John 12:32 is one of the most important statements ever made by Jesus. He reproved the Pharisees for shutting up the kingdom of heaven against men. "*Woe unto you, Scribes and Pharisees, hypocrites! For ye shut up the kingdom of heaven against men; for ye neither go in yourselves, nor suffer ye them that are entering to go in*" (**Matt. 23:13**).

They were never guilty of shutting up the kingdom of hell – they were perfectly willing that it should be kept open, and that many should go in there; but the door of the kingdom of heaven they endeavored to close against all who did not think and do as they did. How many there are at this day just like the Scribes and Pharisees of old! They open hell and shut heaven to most of humanity.

If Jesus were on earth, He would say to them, "*Woe unto you!*" as He did unto their ancient brethren. Remember, elsewhere Christ said to his disciples, "*Beware of the doctrine of the Scribes and Pharisees*" (**Mk. 12:38**). Jesus labored, preached, suffered, died, rose from the dead, and ascended on high, that all might enter his kingdom; and we are informed, "*He shall see of the travail of his soul, [and] shall be satisfied: by his knowledge shall my righteous servant justify* [the] *many; for he shall bear their* [obviously, all humankind's] *iniquities*" (**Is. 53:11**, KJV). All humanity, then, will finally enter the kingdom of heaven. -- [MANFORD & MARSHALL]

Ez. 33:11   HOPE FOR WICKED TO TURN BACK

"'*As I live,*' declares my Lord, Yahweh, '*I delight not in the death of the wicked, but rather that the wicked one turn back from his way and live.*'"

"These words come right from God's heart and they clearly display His attitude. In their evil doings, the Israelites faced the wage of SIN, which is "death." No mention was made to the Israelites, however, of a permanent judgment in hell for those who died in SIN. since this verse proves that God is in a state of displeasure when wicked people die, will He choose to be unhappy forever by consigning them to "eternal death?" If this were so, He would mean He intends to remain permanently disgruntled, even though He has the power to train, educate, and reform lost sinners after death! Although Ezekiel 33:11 does not mention the hereafter, poignant questions arise from it concerning the validity of the "limited atonement" theory." -- [G. HOWE]

Micah 7:18, 19   NOT HOLDING ANGER FOREVER

Micah said, of Yahweh, "Who *is an El (God) as you are, bearing (putting up with) depravity, and passing over transgressions, for the remnant of His allotment? He does not hold fast His anger for the future, for He delights in kindness. He will return, having compassion on us. He will subdue depravities. And you wilt fling into the shadowy depths of the sea all our sins."* (CLV)

RE-INTERPRETATION: "Who is a God [a forgiver] like unto thee, which pardons all of humanity's depravities, iniquity, and even passing over transgressions of the remnant of His allotment? He retains not His anger beyond the end of all the ages, because He (ultimately) delighteth in (universal) mercy for all humanity. He WILL turn again, and WILL have compassion upon the descendants of Adam; He WILL subdue all of humanity's depravities and iniquities; and WILL cast ALL humankind's imperfections into the depths of the sea."

"Who is like this great forgiver of all humankind? It surely is not the 'limited atonement' church dogmatists of today. Verse 20 and the first part of verse 18 deals with God's faithfulness to Jacob and Abraham and how God has removed the iniquities of the Israelite remnant. This fact may cause some critics to limit these and other promises in the Old Testament to the Jews only. Doing this, however, neglects the "first-fruit" concept practice of the Old Testament together with its New Testament application by James (1:18). James wrote that believers in Christ are a first-fruit of the whole creation, meaning all humankind. Careful adoption of this promise prepares us for the blessings God will finally shed upon all people. Micah 7:18b-19 demonstrates that God delights in kindness, not in judgement. Through the infinite work of Christ, God the Father is able to subdue our iniquities and cast all SIN into the depths of the sea." -- [G. HOWE]

"This verse with its context stands directly in support of universalism, inasmuch as it declares that God pardoneth all iniquity and passeth by the transgression of the remnant of his heritage. On this, Dr. Clarke remarks: "Nothing can please Him (God) better, than having the opportunity, from the return and repentance of the sinner, to show him that mercy without which He must perish everlastingly." -- [AUSTIN]

This is a most precious assurance altogether at variance with the doctrine of endless misery!

Ps. 103:6-14   WILL NOT ACCUSE FOREVER

" *Yahweh is the One doing righteousness and justice for all of the ones being oppressed. The Lord is compassionate and gracious, slow to anger and abundant in unfailing love. He will not always accuse and He will not hold on to His anger* (forever) *for the eon. He did not do to us after our sins nor did He treat us according to our iniquities, for He knows our frame, being mindful that we are dust.*"

Psalm 103:7 and 11-13 carry specific ties to Israel. But verses 6, 8-10, and 14, have reference to "all" people of all time and all places, as in the phrase "all of the ones being oppressed." His unfailing love, His refusal to harbor indignation beyond the age, and His recognition of human frailties all rise to refute the orthodox belief that God's judgments last forever.

Ps. 86:15   GOD SLOW TO ANGER

"*And you, my God, compassionate and gracious God, slow to anger, and abundant in unfailing love and faithfulness!*"

"This needs no comment, for it is impossible for such a being to torment without relief, and without end, millions of his own offspring." -- [MANFORD}

In the verse just before this one (Psalm 86:14) David reported that He was being attacked by arrogant, ungodly, and ruthless men who wanted to kill him. What a contrast David drew between those evil enemies and God Himself! In verses 15-16 David committed the whole crisis to God and asked for merciful deliverance. David understood personally that God is slow to indignation and that even His discipline is permeated by unfailing love. -- [HOWE]

Heb. 8:10, 12   ALL SINS FORGOTTEN

"*For this is the covenant that I shall make with... Israel, after those days, I shall be propitious to their (Israel's) injustices, and their sins and their lawlessness should I under no circumstances still be reminded.*"

Since, Paul says, 'the Body of Christ' is (for now, during the Grace Age) 'the true Israel of God' **(Gal. 6: 16)**, and that God promises to save ALL Israel, we can say that this verse, in a much broader sens includes ALL THE GENTILES. For example, "This is the new reconciliation promise that I have now made, with the house of Adam-kind, after those days of Christ Crucified, I am now being merciful to all humans, because there is now no difference between Jew and Greek (or Gentile). Therefore, humanity's transgressions and iniquities I will remember no more, when the Great Day of reconciliation comes."

Is. 1:18   FORGIVENESS FOR THE WORST SINS

"*If your sins be as double scarlet, as snow shall they be white. If they are reddened as crimson, as wool shall they become.*"

'Your' = "all of humanity." The greatest and blackest SIN, then, can be removed from the human soul. Eternity will never reveal the time when this cannot be done. How false is the creed that says a large part of humankind will soon be placed beyond the reach of redeeming grace! -- [MANFORD].

Ps. 103:3   ALL THE WORLD'S SIN PARDONED

"*Who forgiveth ALL thine [mankind's] iniquities; who healeth ALL thy [mankind's] diseases.*"

Jer. 33:8   WILL PARDON ALL INIQUITIES

"*I WILL cleanse them [Israel & all Gentile descendants] from ALL their iniquities, whereby they have committed violations against me; and I WILL pardon ALL their iniquities, whereby they have sinned [transgressed against God], and whereby they have transgressed against me.*"

All men are oppressed by what Adam did. Thus, "*The LORD executes righteousness and judgment for ALL those who are (and have been, and will be) oppressed*"**(Ps. 103: 6, 19)**. God has prepared His throne in the heavens, and His kingdom rules over ALL. This includes the entire human race.

Eph. 1:7   FORGIVENESS OF ALL OFFENSES

"*...in whom we are having the deliverance through His blood, the forgiveness of offenses in accord with the riches of His grace.*"

"In whom we (all humans) have redemption through His blood, the forgiveness of our sins (and the removal of Adamic condemnation), according to the riches of his grace." KJV with interpretations.

Acts 13:38   ALL MANKIND PARDONED OF SINS

"*Let it then be known to you, men, brethren [humankind as a whole] that through this One [man] is being announced to you [to the ends of the earth, to all mankind] the pardon of sins.*" (CLV with interpretations)

This verse appears to be talking to those who are 'hearing the gospel' maybe for the first time, as it is 'being announced' to them, who are then, called 'brethren' by the writer of Acts. The message to them is the pardoning of all sins.

1 Cor. 15:22   ALL THE DEAD RAISED IN CHRIST AND GIVEN LIFE

and **Rom. 5:12**, also **1 Cor. 15:42-44, 49, 51-53**.]

"*As in Adam ALL* [descendants of Adam] *die, even so in Christ* [the second Adam] *WILL ALL* [of Adam's descendants] *be made alive.*"(KJV with interpretations)

"*Therefore, even as through one (human) man SIN entered into the world, and through SIN death, and thus death passed through into all mankind, on which all sinned...*" (CLV)

This is a very important passage. It teaches universal death and universal life. All die, and all shall live again. All the dead, all who die in Adam, shall be raised in Christ; none shall be raised out of him, but all in him. Paul draws the parallel lines between the first and 2ed Adam and between the extent of natural and moral death on the one hand, and of immortal and spiritual life on the other. He shows that all who had or would experience the former, should eventually experience the latter.

The apostle's language is so clear and full with respect to the final happiness of those who are thus raised, and that their resurrection to life will be ultimately a blessing. Christian tradition has falsely supposed that He is here treating of the resurrection of the virtuous only. That is not the fact, for He evidently speaks of the restoration of the entire human race. Christ shall raise all who die by Adam; otherwise, the apostle's assertion would be untrue. The case then would have been this: as in Adam all die, so in Christ shall a select number, a small proportion, be made alive. However, this is not the apostle's doctrine. His expressions are equally universal in each clause. ALL die in Adam. The same ALL, without any exception, without any restriction, shall by Christ be restored to life, and ultimately to holiness and everlasting happiness.

Tradition teaches that the resurrection spoken of here is a resurrection of the body merely. It is, therefore, only a physical change and does not imply that everyone who will be thus raised will be saved. There is good evidence that many shall be raised but not to redemption. How do men die in Adam? Adam here signifies earthy man. Every man is an earthy man.

Well, as in the earthy man all die, even so in Christ (the heavenly man) shall all be made alive. Now, how do men die in the earthy man? They die both physically and morally. Rom. 5:12, says, *"By one man SIN entered into the world, and death by SIN; and so death passed upon all men, and because of that all have sinned."* Natural death is the result of a mortal constitution, which every man has. Moral death is the result of SIN, which every man commits. Well, as in the earthy man, all die physically and morally, even so in Christ shall all be made alive physically and morally. Besides, the apostle shows that all who are raised from the state of death will be raised from *"corruption to incorruption,"* from *"dishonor to glory."*

This certainly shows that the change to be effected by the resurrection is something more than a mere physical change. Nor does the apostle give the least hint or intimation, in the whole chapter that any who are raised will be miserable thereafter. On the contrary, He speaks of it as a change to be effected upon all humankind, and upon all alike.

2 Cor. 5:17 ALL RECEIVE SALVATION

All who are in Christ are recipients of salvation, said the same writer,

"If any man be in Christ, He is a new creature, old things are passed away, and behold all things are become new."

This is the blessed state of all who are and ever will be in Christ. They are in possession of the salvation of heaven. Do not forget the promise is that all who die in Adam shall be thus blessed.

Rom. 8:1 ALL FREED FROM CONDEMNATION

"There is no condemnation to them that are in Christ Jesus."

They are also free from condemnation. All the dead are to be raised bearing the image of the heavenly. *"So also is the resurrection of the dead* (of all who die in Adam). *It was sown in corruption, it is to be raised in incorruption; it was sown in dishonor, it is to be raised in glory; it was sown in weakness, it is to be raised in power; it was sown a natural body, it is to be raised a spiritual body. There is a natural body, and there is a spiritual body... And as we have borne the image of the earthy, we shall also bare the image of the heavenly"* (I Cor. 15:42-44, 49).

Let it not be forgotten that the Apostle is here speaking of a universal resurrection of all who die in Adam. Of this, there can be no doubt. That act is prominent through the whole of this highly important chapter. A blessed immortality then for all humankind is established beyond all doubt, all cavil. The writer, in the same chapter, repeats the same soul-inspiring truth. *"The dead (all who die in Adam) shall be raised incorruptible, and we shall be changed. For this corruption must put on incorruption, and this mortal must put on immortality"* (I Cor. 15: 52).

The Apostle again teaches that the change from earthly to heavenly is to be universal. "Behold I show you a mystery; we shall not all sleep, but we shall all be changed in a moment, in the twinkling of an eye, at the last trump; for the trumpet shall sound, and the dead shall be raised incorruptible, and we shall be changed" (I Cor. 15: 51, 52). Dr. Clarke understands this to refer to all mankind. He says, the "resurrection of all the dead, from the foundation of the world to that time, and the change of all the living then upon the earth, shall be the work of a single moment."

The change, then, is to be universal – the living and the dead are to be changed. But notwithstanding this plain testimony, it is supposed by some there is to be no change after death; that during the countless ages of eternity, all will retain the same characters they possessed when they breathed their last breath and heaved their last sigh in this world – a doctrine at variance with reason, benevolence and the word of God. If it is true, but few will participate in the joys of heaven, for nearly all of humanity live and die, more or less sinful. However, this is not true. All who die in Adam are to be made alive in Christ. -- [MANFORD]

1 Cor. 15:42-44, 49, 51, 52, 53   ALL BEAR THE IMAGE OF THE CELESTIAL

"*So also is the resurrection of the dead (of all who die in Adam). It is sown in corruption, it is raised in incorruption; it is sown in dishonor, it is raised in glory; it is sown in weakness, it is raised in power; it is sown a natural body, it is raised a spiritual body. There is a natural body, and there is a spiritual body, and as we have borne the image of the earthy, we shall also bare the image of the heavenly.*"

All the dead are to be raised, bearing the image of the heavenly. Let it not be forgotten that the Apostle is here speaking of a universal resurrection of all who die in Adam. Of this, there can be no doubt. That act is prominent through the whole of this highly important chapter. A blessed immortality then for all humankind is established beyond all doubt, all cavil. The writer, in the same chapter, repeats the same soul-inspiring truth. "*The dead* (all who die in Adam) *shall be raised incorruptible, and we shall be changed. For this corruption must put on incorruption, and this mortal must put on immortality*" (I Cor. 15: 52, 53).

The Apostle again teaches that the change from earthly to heavenly is to be universal. "Behold I show you a mystery; we shall not all sleep, but we shall all be changed in a moment, in the twinkling of an eye, at the last trump; for the trumpet shall sound, and the dead shall be raised incorruptible, and we shall be changed" (I Cor. 15: 51, 52).

Dr. Clarke understands this to refer to all mankind. He says, the "resurrection of all the dead, from the foundation of the world to that time, and the change of all the living then upon the earth, shall be the work of a single moment." The change, then, is to be universal – the living and the dead are to be changed. But notwithstanding this plain testimony, it is supposed by some there is to be no change after death; that during the countless ages of eternity, all will retain the same characters they possessed when they breathed their last breath and heaved their last sigh in this world – a doctrine at variance with reason, benevolence and the word of God. If it is true, but few will participate in the joys of heaven, for nearly all of mankind live and die, more or less sinful. However, it is not true; all who die in Adam are to be made alive in Christ. -- [MANFORD]

Rom. 8:20, 21   ALL RETURN TO GOD AND DELIVERED FROM CORRUPTION

"*For the creature was made subject to vanity, not willingly, but by reason of him who hath subjected the same in hope; because the creation itself WILL be delivered from the bondage of corruption into the glorious liberty of the children of God.*" - KJV

The word 'creation' in this passage necessarily includes "every human creature," or "ALL mankind."

1 Cor. 15:28   ALL SUBDUED WITH GOD ALL IN ALL

"*And when all things shall be subdued unto him, then shall the Son also himself be subject unto him that put all things under him, that God may be ALL IN ALL.*"

"God is love" and so in the resurrection state all will be redeemed from the dominion of SIN, and be imbued with love divine. What a blessed promise! What a glorious theme for contemplation! Love will triumph over all opposing obstacles and enthrone itself in every heart. Then will the purpose of God relative to man's destiny, be consummated; then will Jesus have performed his Father's will. -- [MANFORD]

1 Cor. 8:6   ALL PEOPLE ARE FROM GOD AND RETURN TO HIM

"*Yet to us [there is but] One God: the Father out of Whom [is] all and we in Him and one Lord Jesus Christ through Whom [is] all and we through Him.*"

While this verse does not discuss or even mention God's final reconciliation of all people, it shows the basis by which reconciliation of all is both possible and logical. If all exists in God and through God, then God owns all. It should not surprise us that God decided to save all people; they are, after all, His possessions!

I Corinthians 8:6 also contains a bold presentation of Jesus Christ as part of the everlasting Godhead. All punctuation marks in English translations are of human origin, there being no such punctuation in the manuscripts. To determine the meaning of, it is suggested that a colon be placed after "One God:" Following that colon, the remainder of the verse then designates two Individuals who are each part of the "One God:" the Father [Who is the Ground of All Being] and the Lord Jesus Christ [Who is the agency or channel through whom all exists]. To punctuate the sentence so that the "One God" remark covers only the Father turns the Lord Jesus

Christ into a Unitarian afterthought. This is not what Paul had in mind. It was Paul's desire to proclaim Jesus Christ as a coexistent and coeternal Deity along with the Father. Punctuating the verse to show otherwise is to set it wrongly in opposition to the rest of scripture and does damage to our understanding of Christ's nature. -- [G. HOWE]

1 Cor. 15:49   ALL OBTAIN THE CELESTIAL IMAGE

See also, 24-28, 42-44, and 51-54. Rom. 11. 36, Heb. 2:8, 9

"And according as we wear the image of the soulish, we should be wearing the image also of the Celestial."

The Apostle Paul teaches that all who have borne or shall bear the image of the earthy man, shall also bear the image of the heavenly man. *"And as we have borne the image of the earthy, we shall also bear the image of the heavenly"* (**1 Cor. 15:49**). Paul teaches the resurrection of all the dead out of corruption and into incorruption, from weakness to power, from natural to spiritual, from dishonor to glory. He teaches the change of both the living and the dead from mortal to immortal. He said, *"So also is the resurrection of the dead; it is sown in corruption, it is raised in incorruption; it is sown in dishonor, it is raised in glory; it is sown in weakness, it is raised in power; it is sown a natural body, it is raised a spiritual body"* (**1 Cor. 15:42-44**). *"Behold, I show you a mystery; we shall not all sleep, but we shall all be changed in a moment, in the twinkling of an eye, at the last trump (for the trumpet shall sound); and the dead shall be raised incorruptible, and we shall be changed. For, the corruptible must put on incorruption, and this mortal must put on immortality. So when this corruptible shall have put on incorruption, and this mortal shall have put on immortality, and then shall be brought to pass the saying that is written* [see **Isa. 25: 6-8**], *Death is swallowed up in victor"* (**1 Cor. 15:51-54**).

It is often asserted that there is no change after death; but, if there is any truth in the declaration of the apostle in these texts, the most important change which will ever be experienced by man will take place after death. Man, therefore, in the resurrection world, will be a very different being from what He is here. All reasoning, then, upon the subject of what man will be there from what He is here, is entirely out of the question. He taught that out of God, as the great author, origin, source, and fountain, all things have proceeded; and that into him, as the great center to which they are tending, shall all things return: "*For of him (God), and through him, and to him, are all things: to whom be glory forever. Amen.*" Needless to say, "Who cannot respond?" (**Rom. 11:36**).

Finally, He teaches the subjection of all intelligent beings to Christ; and, finally, there and Christ's subjection to God; that God may become the all and in all of his creatures. "*Then cometh the end, when He (Christ) shall have delivered up the kingdom to God, even the Father; when He shall have put down all rule, and all authority and power. For He must reign until be hath put all enemies under his feet. The last enemy that shall be destroyed is death, for He hath put all things under his feet. Now, when He saith, all things are put under him; it is manifest that He is accepted, which did put all things under him. And, when all things shall be subdued unto him, then shall the Son also himself be subject unto him that did put all things under him that God may be all in all*"(**Cor. 15:24-28**).

This testimony very plainly asserts the following facts. 1.) All things, that is, all beings, are to be brought into subjection to Christ. This work is now going on. It is a progressive work, but will eventually be consummated.

In **Heb. 2:8, 9**, Paul says, "*Thou (God) hast put all things in subjection under his* (Christ's) *feet, for in that He put all in subjection tinder him, He left nothing that is not put under him. Now we see not yet all things put under him. But we see Jesus, who was made a little lower than the angels for the suffering of death, crowned with glory and honor that He by the grace of God should taste death for every man.*" 2.) There is but one exception to this universal subjection, and that exception is God. 3.) Christ is to put down all rule, and all authority and power. Of course, when this is accomplished, the devil will have no rule, nor authority, nor power. 4.) Christ and all mankind are finally to become subject to the power, the authority, and the government of God.

We have shown that mankind is not only to become subject to God, but is to be reconciled to him. Of course, there will then be no rebels against God in the universe; either in will, wish, desire, or action; but the spirit of God, Who is love, will pervade the hearts and minds of all his creatures, and He himself become all in all. Then God's will and purpose respecting the final destiny of his creatures will be accomplished. His promises will be fulfilled, his oath performed, and his counsel established. Christ will see of the travail of his soul, and be satisfied; and the highest and holy wishes and desires of the hearts of all God's rational creatures will be gratified.

Ps. 68:18   ALL THE REBELLIOUS GIFTED

"*You ascend to the heights. You take captivity captive. You apportion gifts to mankind, and even to the rebellious ones, that You, O Lord, may tabernacle.*"

Most English translations have an error in **Psalm 68:18**. Where the Hebrew says that God apportioned (or gave) gifts to mankind, the translators mistakenly said that God received gifts from mankind. When Paul quoted **Psalm 68:18 in Ephesians 4:8,** He plainly wrote that God gave the gifts. Since He intends to dwell, to tabernacle, or to rest among all people, the Lord will supply gifts to them, even to the stubborn or refractory individuals, who will by that time be changed. God's universal approach in giving gifts to all people, even the rebellious ones, is well substantiated in scriptures such as **Lk. 6:35-36.** Likewise, Paul taught that God would have mercy even on people who cannot be convinced or persuaded (**Romans 11:32**). In **Ephesians 4:8,** Paul applied **Psalm 68:18** to God's giving various spiritual gifts to Christian believers. It is interesting that God will enslave captivity itself, a remark that proves He will not use everlasting captivity to punish those who "*die in their sins.*" -- [G. HOWE]

James 1:18   ALL MADE NEW CREATURES

"*Of His own WILL He beat us [each one as they come to believe] with the word of truth, that we [i.e. those that especially believe] should be a kind of first-fruits of His creatures.*" - KJV with interpretations.

ALL ENEMIES MADE FOOTSTOOLS

All men who are believers are "in Christ" and are God's friends. All men that are not one of the "*especially those that believe*" are God's enemies, or we should say, His adversaries. Yet, we may correctly say that they all will be "in Christ" later, when He makes them His footstool. Some verses highly suggest that the phrase "in Christ" means "***in the Work of Christ***" God will have all mankind be vivified and given life. "*For even as, in Adam, all are dying, thus also, in Christ, shall all be vivified*" (**1 Cor. 15:22. CLV**). And, "*The LORD said unto my Lord, sit thou at my right hand, until I make thine enemies thy footstool*" (**Ps. 110:1, Mt. 22:24, Heb. 10:13, Acts 2:35, and Lk. 20:43**). The Lord tells us that His enemies shall be made His

93

"*footstool*" and that includes all the Earth and its inhabitance. For, "*Thus saith the LORD, The heaven [is] my throne, and the earth [is] my footstool* " (**Is. 66:1**). Moreover, "*the earth is God's footstool*" (**Matt. 5:35**).

Now, the Ark is also called his footstool, because it is under the mercy seat (**Ps. 82**), between the cherubim; this was the most sacred of all symbols of God's presence. It is called his "*footstool*" (**1 Chron. 28**). A golden footstool is mentioned in **2 Chron. 9: 18** and is attached to His throne, whose magnificence is described as unrivaled. Another positive reference to footstools is the house as a place of rest for the ark of the covenant. It is called a footstool (**1 Chron.28:2**)

These few verses refer to the '*footstool* as a positive element in God's economy as opposed to what we have been taught. To be made a footstool is apparently to be regenerated into some new identity and one of greatly favored value. God's purpose for creating some evil and wicked was probably so that He may "**work**" them all to the good in becoming His footstool later.

The earth was corrupt and full of SIN, yet God refers to it as being His footstool. God's enemies are corrupt and full of SIN just as were believers, "*while we were yet sinners*," but He makes a promise to subdue all His enemies and make them His footstool. Is this not a good thing? Is there anything He does not work toward goodness for the sake of those who love the Lord? Do we see any other definition for footstool other than one of goodness and usefulness?

After reviewing these verses we see that God reconciles or "*turns*" all His enemies (all evil, corrupt, fallen, sinful people) into His a prized, valued, and even possibly "golden" footstool. He, as a carpenter, "reconstructs" his enemies from adverse, evil, corrupt sinners into beautiful footstools. Apparently, the turning of enemies into footstools refers to a universal reconciling of humanity, even for the most advanced of sinners.

This is the teaching in Scripture that God has given Christ ownership of all things, even His worse enemies. This is done through, is accomplished by and for Christ, by Him drawing all men towards and into reconciliation in His resurrection: "*And I, if I be lifted up from the earth, will draw all [men] unto me*"(**Jn 12:32**). The word means "when" or "since," for Christ surely knew He was going to rise up with no "ifs," "ands,""buts," "maybes," "mights" or doubts about it.

God loves His enemies (Matt. 5:44) and demands that we do as well, even to pray for them while they curse us (**Lk. 6:28, 36, Matt. 5:44, 48 and Lk. 6:27, 36; Matt. 5:44, 46**) and even bless them in our prayers (**Rom. 12:14-18**). As He feeds both the good and the wicked, so we are told to do so in likeness of Him (**Rom. 12:20 and Prov. 25:21**). This is His way to overcome evil with good by not exchanging evil for evil (**Rom. 12:17, 19**), for showing partiality is sinful (**Jam. 2:8-9**). He forgives 490 times plus (**Matt. 18:21-22**) in working all to restoration, whether they be meek or wicked (**Gal. 6:1**) and this should be our way too (**Rom. 12:21; 1 Pet. 3:8-11**). We are to have mercy as He shows mercy (**Prov. 3:3**) and to understand that He is reconciling even His enemies and all the wicked (**Rom. 5:10; Col. 1:21**). Truly, God is turning all that is negative into His footstools.

Ps. 110:1

"Jehovah declared to my Lord, 'Sit at my right hand <u>until I shall set</u> the ones who are Your enemies as a stool for Your feet."

Psalm 110:1 is quoted in **Acts 2:34-35**. Mention is also made three other times in the New Testament of God's enemies being changed into His footstool. There is no discussion of great military subjugation by which the enemies are crushed and then put under the Lord's feet. It is said instead that God will "set" (*sit,* transliterated Hebrew) them as a footstool. Evidently, reconstructive changes will put God's enemies into a peaceful and helpful relationship with the Lord. Psalm 110:1 highlights the identity of two of the three Partners within the eternal Trinity: God the Father and God the Son, since it recorded a comment made by One to the Other. - [G. HOWE]

OTHER REFERENCE SOURCES

THE UNIVERSALIST BELIEF: Or The Doctrinal Views or Universalists. By Rev. Asher Moore. This is a work of great merit, and one which has been eagerly sought after. The first edition was speedily disposed of, and the publisher has been Hnable to supply many orders which have recently been received. It is written in a chaste and forcible style, and furnishes as clear an exposition of, and convincing argument for the main points of our faith as any book ever issued from our press.

UNIVERSALISM, The Doctrine Of The Bible.— Bv Key. Asher Moore. This work is written in the author's very best style, and will, we hare no doubt, be considered one of the most able works ever written in defence of the final holiness and happiness of all mankind.

LECTURES TO YOUTH. By Rev. Stephen R. Smith. This book is entirely free from sectarianism. It is written in a very beautiful style, and inculcates throughout its pages the purest lessons of virtue, the true foundation of all religion.

HYMNS OF ZION : With Appropriate Music. By Rev. A. C. Thomas.

THE SELECT THEOLOGICAL LIBRARY. This is a series of valuable Universalist Books, printed in the cheap form with a view of an extensive circulation. Each work is printed without abridgement, in book style, on fine white paper, with new Brevier type, in a neat and handsome manner, and enclosed in a well printed and appropriate cover. Some of the most useful Universalist Books are furnished in this style at about onefourth the price for which they have heretofore been sold. These books are sold so extremely low, and the beneficial influence they are calculated to exert is so very great, that it is hoped their publication will so far receive the approval of Universalists as to induce each one to buy several of them, and distribute them gratuitously among those of opposing sects. Persons residing in country places can derive much advantage from these publications—for beside their extreme cheapness, they can be sent to any part of the country at the bare cost of periodical postage.

THE UNIVERSAL RESTORATION : exhibited in Four Dialogues between a Minister and his Friend; comprehending the substance of several real conversations which the author had with various persons, both in America and Europe, on that interesting subject; chiefly designed fully to state and fairly to answer the most common objections that are brought against'it from the Scriptures. By Elhanan WinChester. To this work is attached a brief Memoir of the Author by Rev. Hosea Ballou, 2nd, D. D.— It is almost unnecessary to say any thing in favor of this excellent book. The fact of its having run through four or five editions at a high price, speaks much in its favor.

THOUGHTS ON THE DIVINE GOODNESS, relative to the Government of Moral Agents, particularly displayed in Future Rewards and Punishments. Translated from the French of Ferdinand Olivier Petitpierre, formerly minister of Chaux-defond. With a Preface by Rev. T. J. Sawyer, A. M. This work is worthy of attentive perusal. It is one of the most pleasing defences of Universal Salvation that was ever published. Petitpierre was not only amiable in his character,-but he was a man of clear intellect, and the traits both of his mind and his affections are plainly seen in this work.

THE TWENTY-FOURTH AND TWENTYFIFTH CHAPTERS OF ST.

MATTHEW'S GOSPEL, illustrated with notes, fyc. By Hosea Ballou, 2nd, D. D. A clear and convincing commentary on one of the most important portions of the New Testament, written by one of 'the ablest Theological writers of the present day.

ILLUSTRATIONS OF THE DIVINE GOVERNMENT. By T. Southwood Smith, M. D. This has universally been regarded as one of the best books in the whole range of our publications, and is one of the very best works in the English language to convince a thinking man of the truth of Universalistn. It has passed through several editions, none of which have ever sold for less than 75 cents but this, which is only 25 cents.

UNION; a Treatise of the Consanguinity and Affinity between Christ and his Church. By James Relly, with a Preface by Rev. A. C. Thomas, and an article on The First Transgression, by Rev. T. F. Kino. This is a rare and interesting work, written in a clear argumentative style, and is well worthy of an attentive perusal. This book is peculiarly interesting to the Universalist denomination, as being the means of leading John Murray to a belief of the doctrine of the final holiness and happiness of all men. "A copy of the Union falling providentially in his way, Mr. Murray was led, step by step, to unwavering trust in God as the Savior of all."

THE RESTORATION OF ALL THINGS: or a Vindication of the Goodness and Grace of God, to be manifested at last in the recovery of his whole creation out of their fall. By Jeremiah White, Chaplain to Oliver Cromwell. With an additional Preface, by Rev. Thomas Whittemore. As its title imports, the sole object of this work is to set up and defend the doctrine of Universal Salvation, which is done entirely upon the ground of the Scriptures, according to the views entertained by the author. He was a Trinitarian, and held the doctrine of future punishment.

TEN LETTERS ADDRESSED TO Mr. PAINE, IN ANSWER TO HIS PAMPHLET ENTITLED THE "AGE OF REASON" : containing some clear and satisfactory evidence of the truth of Divine Revelation; and especially of the Resurrection and .Ascension of Jesus. By Elhanan Winchester. This is an able refutation of Paine's celebrated Age of Reason, and is one of the very best of the productions of its eminent author. We not only have all the arguments of Paine completely destroyed, but we have an able and eloquent vindication of the truths of Divine Revelation, and of the resurrection of Jesus Christ.

THE EVERLASTING GOSPEL, commanded to be preached by Jesus Christ, Judge of the Living and Bead, unto all creatures, (Mark 16 : 15^ concerning the Eternal Redemption found out by him, whereby Devil, Sin, Hell, and Death, shall at last be abolished, and the whole creation be restored to its primitive purity; being a testimony against the present anti-christian world. By Paul Seigvolk. This work contains a great amount of thought, and some of the clearest and most scriptural views of the Divine character and government, and is the book that first led the celebrated Elhanan Winchester to embrace Universalism. Mr. Winchester says, "It was the first book that ever I saw which treated upon the subject of the Universal Restoration, and it was by reading a little therein that I first began to turn my thoughts and attention to the system which I now hold. Indeed the arguments pressed upon my mind in such a manner that I could not get rid of them : and though I strove long against them, yet they conquered me in about three years. I cannot help therefore having a great regard for this work, as it proved the first means of my conviction, and at length brought me to embrace this most glorious and universal plan of salvation, through Jesus Christ our Lord."

OPINIONS AND PHRASEOLOGY OF THE JEWS, CONCERNING A FUTURE STATE ; from the time of Moses, to that of their final dispersion, by the

Romans. By Hosea Ballou, 2nd, D. D.

THE ARGUMENT FOR THE ABOLITION OF CAPITAL PUNISHMENT, in twelve essays. The two above named works are put under the same cover. The first is from the pen of one so well known to the Universalist denomination, that the appearance of his name on the title will secure it a welcome wherever it maybe received. The other, "Essays on Capital Punishment," is the production of a gentlemen of this city, whose talents and acquirements are the admiration of all who know him. It is probable that these essays contain a clearer and more extensive view of the subject discussed, than can be found in any other work now before the public.

FAMILIAR CONVERSATIONS, in which the Salvation of all mankind is clearly exhibited and illustrated ; and the most ^important objections which are now brought against the doctrine, are fairly stated and fully answered. By Russell Streeter. This work is too well known to the Universalist public to need much commendation here. It has already gone through two large editions, and the third has been for some time loudly called for. And we are sure that nothing could be published more welcome to our denomination, or more useful to our cause.

UNVERSALISM AGAINST PARTIALISM. By Woodbury M. Fernald. This is a modern work, an edition of which was recently published, and rapidly sold in Boston. The unusual demand for it since it has been out of print, as well as the intrinsic merit of the work itself, has induced the publishers to obtain the privilege of issuing it in the cheap form. It is a powerful refutation of the doctrine of endless punishment, and a clear exposition and defence of Universalism.

SELECT THEOLOGICAL LIBRARY. This work contains The Universal Restoration, by Elhanan Winchester; Thoughts on the Divine Goodness, by Ferdinand Olivier Petitpierre ; The Twentyfourth and Twenty-fifth Chapters of St. Matthew's Gospel, illustrated with notes by II. Ballou, 2d; Illustrations of the Divine Government, by T. Southwood Smith; Union, by James Relly ; The First Transgression, by T. F. King; The Restoration of All Things, by Jeremiah While. It has received the unqualified recommendation of the conductors of every Universalist press in the country, as well as of almost, if not every clergyman, and a vast number of the laymen of our denomination. The style in which it is issued, the character of the works published, and the terms for which it is furnished, have all met with general approbation.

THE UNIVERSALIST EXPOSITOR. Edited by Hosea Ballot; and Hosea Ballou, 2nd. 2 vols. 8vo. This is a reprint of a truly valuable work, and contains some of the most valuable writings ever produced by Universalists. It is page for page with the original edition, and furnished at only half the cost. Each volume contains 384 large octavo pages, neatly done up in a paper cover, and is sold at one dollar a volume, or one dollar and seventy-five cents for the two volumes. Those who wish to obtain this standard work, and no family should be without it, must procure it early, as only a small edition has been published.

THE PLAIN GUIDE TO UNIVERSALISM: designed for inquirers to the belief of that Doctrine, and believers to the practice of it. By Rev. Thomas Whittemore.

NOTES AND ILLUSTRATIONS OF THE PARABLES OF THE NEW TESTAMENT, arranged according to the time in which they were spoken. By Rev. Thomas Whittemore.

SKINNER'S DOCTRINAL SERMONS.—^ Series of Sermons in Defence of the Doctrine of Universal Salvation. By Rev. Otis A. Skinner.

AN EXAMINATION OF THE DOCTRINE OF FUTURE RETRIBUTION, in connexion with the Moral Nature of Man, the principle of Analogy and the sacred Scriptures. By Rev. H. Ballou.

NOTES ON THE PARABLES OF THE NEW TESTAMENT, Scripturally illustrated and afgumentatively defended. .By Rev. H. Ballou.

A TREATISE ON THE ATONEMENT; in which the Finite Nature of Sin is argued, its cause and consequences as such; the necessity vnd nature of atonement and its glorious consequences, in the Final Restoration of all men to Holiness and Happiness. By Rev. Hosea Ballou.

DISCOURSES ON VARIOUS SUBJECTS. By Rev. E. H. Chapin.

ORTHODOXY AS IT IS; or its Monial Influence and Practical Inefficiency and Effects Illustrated by Philosophy and Facts. By Rev's. R. Tomlinson, and D P. Livermorb.

THE LAYMAN'S LEGACY, or Fifty Sermons on important subjects. By Henry Fitz. 2 vols.

A DISCUSSION of the conjoint question, Is the Doctrine of Endless Punishment taught in the Bible ! Or does the Bible teach the Final Holiness and Happiness of all Mankind ? By Rev. Dr. Ezra Stiles Ely, Presbyterian, and Rev. Abel C. Thomas, Universalist.

ILLUSTRATIONS OF THE LAW OF KINDNESS. By Rev. George W. Montgomery.

A VOICE TO THE MARRIED: being a compendium of Social, Moral, and Religious Duties, addressed to Husbands and Wives. By Rev. John M. Austin.

AN ARGUMENT FOR CHRISTIANITY. By Rev. I. D. Williamson.

AN EXPOSITION AND DEFENCE OF UNIVERSALISM. By Rev. I. D. Williamson.

ALLEGORIES AND DIVERS DAY DREAMS.— By Rev. Abel C. Thomas.

THE BOOK OF PROMISES ; or the Universalist's Daily Pocket Companion, being a collection of Scripture Promises, arranged under their proper heads. By S. S. Bulfinch Emmons.

SELECTIONS FROM EMINENT COMMENTATORS, who have believed in Endless Punishment, and who agree with Universalists in the Interpretation of Scripture relating to Punishment. By Rev. Lucius R. Paige.

control and use us. There are many theories. The truth is shown in STELLAR STERILITY that man IS ALONE and the only way off this planet is in a box! It also shows that there are NO alien artifacts on our planetary bodies either. It proves beyond a doubt that man is trapped on earth doing "time." Yes, the universe was created for us and us alone, but humans were never meant to inherit it as mortals. This book shows the reader that for man to colonize and inherit the universe he will have to be Immortal and Incorruptible. And, there is only ONE way we are going to do this and aliens aren't it! Read why NASA says we may never leave our solar system! Read also why it is highly unlikely that any aliens have visited us. Maybe there aren't any? Over 600+ pages of shocking scientific evidence and 100's of pictures and illustrations. CreateSpace eStore: https://www.createspace.com/4958613

CONTACT:

ROSS MARSHALL
POB 1191
ANACORTES, WA. 98221

www.WeirdVideos.com
www.UniversalAtonement.com
www.GodSavesAll.org

Made in the USA
Charleston, SC
24 November 2015